super cute
crochet
for
LITTLE FEET

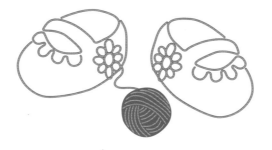

Super Cute Crochet for Little Feet
Copyright © 2014 Quantum Publishing Ltd

www.stmartins.com

First U.S. Edition: March 2015

Library of Congress Cataloging-in-
Publication Data Available Upon Request

ISBN 978-1-250-05910-9

QUMSCCF

This book was designed and produced by
Quantum Publishing
6 Blundell Street
London N7 9BH

Publisher: Sarah Bloxham
Project Manager: Hazel Eriksson
Editor: Anna Southgate
Design: Blanche Williams at
Harper Williams Ltd.
Lifestyle Photography: Vita Apala
Model Photography: Sussie Bell
Model: Isla Campbell
Production Manager: Rohana Yusof

Printed in China by 1010 Printing International

10 9 8 7 6 5 4 3 2 1

super cute
crochet
for
LITTLE FEET

30 stylish shoes, booties, and
sandals to crochet for babies

Vita Apala

St. Martin's Griffin
New York

contents

introduction

Crafting is something I have enjoyed for many years. I learned to crochet when I was very young, having been taught by my grandmother. A little later my mother taught me to knit and I abandoned crochet for some time to concentrate on that. When I became a mother, I found that I had more time and inspiration for crafts than ever before, and it was around this time that I returned to crochet. I have not been able to put down my crochet hook since.

Needless to say, crochet is addictive. It is also very practical with small kids around. All the work you do involves just one loop and one hook, so there is less chance of a project becoming seriously damaged if it finds its way into tiny "helping" hands. Another benefit is that crochet works up much faster than knitting, which, for busy moms, is essential.

I have always loved creating my own designs. I began to share some of my projects online and received so much interest in them that I started to write my own patterns more regularly. This is when and how Mon Petit Violon shop and blog was created.

In this book you will find 30 projects for baby booties for all seasons and every occasion. All patterns are based on adult styles, so you can expose your children to fashion from the cradle, and easily coordinate matching outfits!

The projects are arranged in three chapters: Shoes, Boots and Sandals. Shoes are the easiest to make and include models for both boys and girls. They are perfect for seasonal changes and cooler days. Boots, though slightly more time-consuming, are still easy to make and are essential for the colder months of the year. Depending on the weather where you live you can make them even warmer by using a

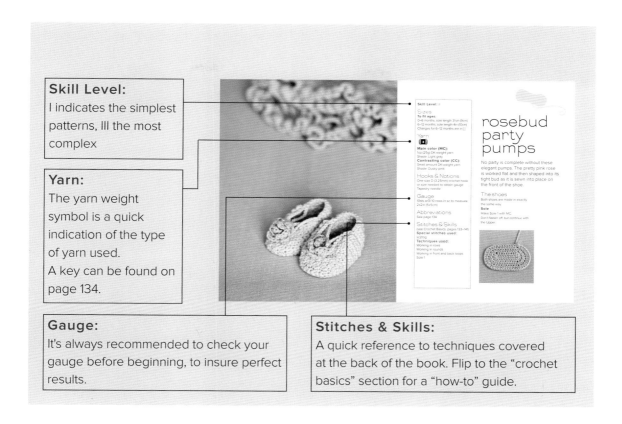

Skill Level:
I indicates the simplest patterns, III the most complex

Yarn:
The yarn weight symbol is a quick indication of the type of yarn used.
A key can be found on page 134.

Gauge:
It's always recommended to check your gauge before beginning, to insure perfect results.

Stitches & Skills:
A quick reference to techniques covered at the back of the book. Flip to the "crochet basics" section for a "how-to" guide.

different type of yarn—alpaca or wool are both very good options. For milder winters, or even summer boots, use cotton or linen. The sandals include some of the more complex projects, but they are worth the effort and are the perfect addition to a baby's summer wardrobe.

The patterns require different skill levels, but many of them are within the ability of a beginner (level I will be the simplest, level III the most challenging). Each pattern has detailed instructions and helpful photos. By following the pattern row by row (or round by round) you will achieve great results and may pick up techniques to use later on in your own projects.

At the back of the book, you'll find instructions on how to make all of the basic stitches and a few special ones that feature in the projects, as well as a list of abbreviations used to describe them. If you have a very active baby who doesn't want to keep his or her shoes on, check out the tips on how to make crocheted shoes stay on better and follow the instructions on how to make a nonslip sole.

I hope you will enjoy these patterns as much as I enjoyed creating them.

Happy crocheting!

Vita Apala

super cute shoes

Bright, cheery, and bursting with pizzazz, these super cute shoes are all set to help your baby stand out in the crowd. From brogues, slip-ons, and moccasins to point shoes, party pumps, and Mary Janes, there's a shoe style here for one and all.

Skill Level: I

Sizes
To fit ages:
0–6 months, sole length 3½in (9cm)
6–12 months, sole length 4in (10cm)
Changes for 6–12 months are in [ ]

Yarn

1oz (25g) DK-weight yarn
Shade: Red

Hooks & Notions
One size D (3.25mm) crochet hook
or size needed to obtain gauge

Gauge
10sts and 10 rows in sc to measure
2x2in (5x5cm)

Abbreviations
see page 134

Stitches & Skills
(see Crochet Basics, pages
133–141)
Special stitches used:
sc2tog
Techniques used:
Working in rows
Working in rounds
Joining in yarn
Sole 1

ballet flats

The ideal choice for a budding dancer, these ballet flats are worked in just one color from the heel of the shoe to the toe. Simply change the yarn color to match a favorite tutu.

The shoes
Both shoes are made in exactly the same way.
Sole
Make Sole 1.
Fasten off.

Upper

Join yarn in st at center back of Sole Heel.

Row 1: ch1, 1sc in st at base of ch-1, 1sc in each of next 45[49]sts, turn.

Rows 2–3: ch1, 1sc in each of next 46[50]sts, turn.

Row 4: ch1, 1sc in each of next 15[17] sts, (skip next st, 1sc in next st) twice, 1sc in each of next 8sts, (skip next st, 1sc in next st) twice, 1sc in each of next 15[17]sts, turn.

Row 5: ch1, 1sc in each of next 14[16] sts, (skip next st, 1sc in next st) twice, 1sc in each of next 6sts, (skip next st,

1sc in next st) twice, 1sc in each of next 14[16]sts, turn.

Row 6: ch1, 1sc in each of next 13[15] sts, (skip next st, 1sc in next st) twice, 1sc in each of next 4sts, (skip next st, 1sc in next st) twice 1sc in each of next 13[15]sts, turn.

Row 7: ch1, 1sc in each of next 12[14] sts, (skip next st, 1sc in next st) twice, 1sc in each of next 2sts, (skip next st, 1sc in next st) twice, 1sc in each of next 12[14]sts, turn.

Row 8: ch1, 1sc in each of next 11[13]sts, (skip next st, 1sc in next st) four times, 1sc in each of next 11[13]sts, turn (see 1). With the wrong side facing (turn inside out) right sides together, place heel side edges, working through both layers, join two halves with sl sts (see 2).

Leaving quite a long tail, join yarn in center front st. Work sl sts around the shoe. Leaving a long tail, fasten off (see 3). Use both tails to tie a bow. Weave in all ends.

Sizes
To fit ages:
0–6 months, sole length 3½in (9cm)
6–12 months, sole length 4in (10cm)
Changes for 6–12 months are in [ ]

Yarn

Main color (MC):
1oz (25g) DK-weight yarn
Shade: Bright green
Contrasting colors (CC):
Small amounts DK-weight yarn
Shades: Cream, yellow

Hooks & Notions
One size D (3.25mm) crochet hook
or size needed to obtain gauge
Tapestry needle

Gauge
10sts and 10 rows in sc to measure
2x2in (5x5cm)

Abbreviations
see page 134

Stitches & Skills
(see Crochet Basics, pages
133–141)
Techniques used:
Working in rows
Working in rounds
Joining in yarn
Sole 1

daisy chain mary janes

With braided straps and daisy buttons,
these bright-green Mary Janes are
simply gorgeous. Who could resist
making a pair for all those garden
parties come summertime?

The shoes
Follow separate instructions for right
and left Uppers.
Sole
Make Sole 1 with MC.
Don't fasten off, but continue with the
right shoe Upper.

Right shoe Upper

With MC.

Rnd 1: ch1, 1sc in each of next 46[50]sts, join with sl st in first sc.

Rnd 2: repeat Rnd 1.

Rnd 3: ch1, 1sc in each of next 6[7]sts, skip next 2sts, 1dc in each of next 14[16]sts, skip next 2sts, 1sc in each of next 22[23]sts, join with sl st into first sc (see 1).

Rnd 4: ch1, 1sc in each of next 6[7]sts, skip next 2sts, 1dc in each of next 10[12]sts, skip next 2sts, 1sc in each of next 22[23]sts, join with sl st into first sc.

Rnd 5: ch1, 1sc in each of next 6[7]sts, *skip next dc, 1sc in next 1dc; repeat from * four[five] times more, 1sc in each of next 8[9]sts, 1hdc in each of next 14sts, join with sl st into first sc.

Rnd 6: ch1, 1sc in each of next 19[22]sts, *skip next st, 1sc in next st; repeat from * six times more, join with sl st into first sc (see 2). Don't fasten off, but continue with strap, as folls: sl st in each of next 2sc, *ch12, 1sc in 2nd ch from hook, 1sc in each foll ch, sl st in next sc (toward Toe); repeat from * twice more. Fasten off (see 3).

tip

The flowers made on page 17 are used as buttons, but if you like you can replace the flower with a pretty button of your choice. Alternatively place a button at the center of the flower and sew the two on together.

Left shoe Upper

Work as for right shoe Upper Rnds 1–6. Fasten off. Continue with strap as folls: Join yarn on opposite side of shoe (see 4), and work *ch12, 1sc in 2nd ch from hook, 1sc in each foll ch, sl st in next sc from ch12; repeat from * twice more. Fasten off (see 5).

For both shoes: Use the three cords you have worked to make a braid. Cut a long thread and stitch the end of the braid to secure.

(see 6). Remove thread from needle and insert hook through one side of braid (where you have the thread), yo, and pull it through (see 7). Now you have a loop. Work ch6, sl st in opposite side of the braid to make a loop (see 8). Turn and work 8sc into the loop. Fasten off (see 9). When braiding the three cords to make the strap, make sure you keep them fairly loose. You still want to be able to see the stitches. This will make for a wider strap, too.

Edging

With CC (cream).

Mark 7 centermost stitches of Toe. With right side facing, join yarn into the st furthest to the right of the marked sts.

Rnd 1: *ch4, sl st in next sc; repeat from * five times more. Fasten off (see 10).

Flower

With CC (yellow).

Foundation ring: ch4, join with sl st.

Rnd 1: ch1, 9sc into ring, change to cream yarn and work 1sl st in 1st ch of round.

Rnd 2: *ch3, sl st in next st; repeat from * around eight times more (nine petals made). Fasten off (see 11). Sew flower onto outside edge of shoe, to align with end of strap and to serve as a button. Weave in all ends.

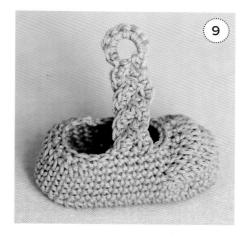

classic slip-ons

When it comes to having a little downtime around the home, what could offer greater comfort than this cute pair of slip-on shoes. Based on an all-time classic design, the color of the uppers can be changed to satisfy any tot's tastes.

The shoes
Both shoes are made in exactly the same way.
Sole
Make Double Sole 1 with CC.
Fasten off.

Row 7: skip 2sl sts, 1sc in each of next 14sts (see 3). Continue with the Back.

Back and Sides
With MC.

Row 1: 1sc in each of next 22[26]sl sts of Sole, sl st in first sc of Front, turn (see 4).

Row 2: skip sl st, 1sc in each of next 22[26]sts, sl st in next sc of Front, turn.

Rows 3–5: repeat Row 2 three times more (see 5).

Row 6: skip sl st, 1sc in each of next 5[6]sts, dc2tog six[seven] times, 1sc in each of next 5[6]sts, sl st in next sc of Front, turn (see 6).

Edging
With MC.

Row 1: skip sl st, 1sc in each of next 16[19]sts, sl st in next st of Front, don't turn but work 1sc in each of next 3sts of Front, 5dc in next st, 1sc in each of next 3sts, sl st in next st (see 7).
Fasten off. Weave in all ends.

tip
You can create your own pattern for the front of the shoe, as long as you keep 14sts as a base. Even something as simple as single crochet instead of FP dc and BP dc will give you a different look.

Skill Level: II

Sizes
To fit ages:
0–6 months, sole length 3½in (9cm)
6–12 months, sole length 4in (10cm)
Changes for 6–12 months are in [ ]

Yarn

1oz (25g) DK-weight yarn
Shade: Pink

Hooks & Notions
One size D (3.25mm) crochet hook
or size needed to obtain gauge
Tapestry needle

Gauge
10sts and 10 rows in sc to measure
2x2in (5x5cm)

Abbreviations
see page 134

Stitches & Skills
(see Crochet Basics, pages
133–141)
Special stitches used:
Shell
Techniques used:
Working in rows
Working in rounds

point shoes

These point shoes are simply stunning—the ideal footwear for a prima donna ballerina. They have no sole, but are worked up from the toe. Make them in soft cream, baby blue, or as here, a light, pastel pink.

The shoes
Both shoes are made in exactly the same way.
Toe
Foundation ring: ch4, join with sl st in first ch.
Rnd 1: ch3 (count as first dc), 23dc into the ring, join with sl st in 3rd ch of ch-3 (see 1).

Rnd 2: ch1, *skip 2sts, shell in next st, skip next 2sts, 1sc in next st; repeat from * three times more, but in last repeat instead of last sc, join with sl st in ch-1. (see 2).

Rnd 3: ch5, 1dc in st at base of ch-5, *1sc in second dc of next shell, shell in next sc; repeat from * twice more, 1sc in second dc of next shell, 1dc in same st as first dc of Rnd 3, ch2, join with sl st in 3rd ch of ch-5.

Rnd 4: ch1, *shell in next sc, 1sc in second dc of next shell; repeat from * three times more, but in last repeat instead of last sc, join with sl st in ch-1. Repeat Rnds 3 and 4 once more for size 0–6 months; twice for 6–12 months (see 3). Don't fasten off, but continue with Heel.

Heel

Row 1: ch1, 1sc in each of the next 18 sts and spaces (the last shell is to be left unworked), turn.

Row 2: ch1, 1sc in each of next 18sts, turn. Repeat Row 2 six times more. Fasten off (see 4).

Heel flap

Join the yarn in 7th stitch from the left-hand heel edge.

Row 1: ch1, 1sc in st at base of ch-1, 1sc in each of next 5sts, sl st in each of next 2sts, turn (see 5).

Row 2: skip 2sl sts, 1sc in each of next 6sc, sl st in each of next 2sc (the ones that remained unworked on side of Heel), turn (see 6).

Rows 3–4: repeat Row 2 twice.

Row 5: skip 2sl sts, 1sc in each of next 6sc, sl st in next sc along edge of Heel, turn.

Row 6: skip sl st, 1sc in each of next 6sc, sl st in next sc along edge of Heel, turn.

Rows 7–8: repeat Row 6 twice more (see 7).

Edging: Round 1: ch1, work 1sc evenly around the shoe, join with sl st in first sc. Fasten off.

Tie

Ch40, 1sc in first st of heel flap (see 8), 1sc in each of next 5sts, ch40. Fasten off. (see 9).
Weave in all ends.

brogues

Complete the wardrobe of a natty dresser with these fabulous two-tone shoes. The heel and toe sections are worked in a contrasting color, replicating perfectly the multipiece construction of the classic design.

The shoes
Both shoes are made in exactly the same way.
Sole
Make a Double Sole 1 with MC.
Fasten off.

Front

With CC. Mark 7 centermost stitches of Toe. With right side facing, join yarn into the st furthest to the right of the marked sts. Working in sl sts worked to join the Soles, continue as folls:

Row 1: ch1, 2sc in base of ch-1, 2sc in each of next 6sts, sl st in each of next 2sl sts along the Sole, turn (see 1, page 20).

Row 2: skip 2sl sts, 1sc in each of next 14sts, skip next sl st of Sole, sl st in next st along the Sole, turn.

Row 3: skip sl st, 1sc in each of next 14sts, skip next sl st, sl st in next st along the Sole, turn. Repeat Row 3 three[five] times more. Fasten off (see 1).

Back and Sides

With MC; for both sizes. Join yarn in st center back of Sole heel (13sts to either side). Working in back loops only of sl sts used to join the Soles.

Rnd 1: ch1, skip st at base of ch-1, 1sc in each of next 13sts, skip sl st, 1sc in first st of Front, 1sc in next st, *along Front sc2tog, 1sc in each of next 2sts; repeat from * twice more, 1sc in each of next 13sts, join with sl st in first sc (see 2).

Rnd 2: ch1, 1sc in each of next 13sts, skip next st, 1sc in each of next 9sts, skip next st, 1sc in each of next 13sts, join with sl st in first sc.

Rnd 3: ch3 (count as first dc), 1dc in each of next 10sts, 1sc in each of next 3sts, skip next st, 1sc in

each of next 7sts, skip next st, 1sc in each of next 3sts, 1dc in each of next 10sts, join with sl st in 3rd ch of ch-3 (see 3).

Rnd 4: ch1, 1sc in each of next 13sts, skip next st, 1sc in each of next 5sts, skip next st, 1sc in each of next 13sts, join with sl st in first sc.

Rnd 5: ch1, 1sc in each of next 13sts, skip next st, 1sc in each of next 3sts, skip next st, 1sc in each of next 13sts, join with sl st in first sc. Fasten off.

Heel

With CC. Join yarn in 6th st Front, and begin. Working in front loop only of the sl sts used to join the Sole to create the Double Sole.

Row 1: ch1, 1sc in st at base of ch-1, 1sc in each of next 16sts, turn (see 4).

Row 2: ch1, skip next st, 1sc in each st until 2 sts remain, skip next st, 1sc in last st, turn.

Rows 3–8: repeat Row 2 six times more. Fasten off. Join the yarn in first st of first row and work 1sc evenly across the row edges of Heel. Fasten off (see 5).

Thread needle with CC and seam Heel to back of shoe with a backstitch seam (see 6).

Take care that you don't work completely through the second layer—this will prevent the seam from being visible.

Weave in all ends. Make a twisted cord measuring 13¾in (35cm) with CC. Use the crochet hook to lace up the front of each shoe.

cutwork shoes

Super sweet, dainty shoes for wearing with lightweight summer outfits. Make them in any color you like and have fun choosing buttons in pretty shapes or with a bit of sparkle.

The shoes
Follow separate instructions for right and left Uppers.
Sole
Make Sole 2.
Don't fasten off, but continue with the right shoe Upper.

Right shoe Upper

Rnd 1: working in back loops only ch1, 1sc in each of next 42[46]sts, join with sl st in first sc.

Rnd 2: working in both loops, ch1, 1sc in each of next 42[46]sts, join with sl st in first sc.

Rnd 3: ch1, 1sc in each of next 9[11]sts, skip next 3sts, CL shell in next st, skip next 3sts, 1sc in each of next 26[28] sts, join with sl st in first sc (see 1).

Rnd 4: ch1, 1sc in each of next 6[8]sts, ch1, skip next 3sc, *skip next CL, sc in next ch3-space, ch1; repeat from * twice more, skip last CL, skip next 3sc,

1sc in each of next 23[25]sts, join with sl st in first sc (see 2).

Rnd 5: ch1, 1sc in each of next 4[5] sts, ch3, skip next 5[6]sts (ch1 counts as stitch), 1sc in next sc, ch3, skip next 5[6]sts (ch1 counts as stitch), 1sc in each of next 21[22]sts, join with sl st in first sc. Continue with the strap, as folls: ch12[14], 1sc in 7th ch from hook, 1sc in each foll ch, sl st in next sc. Fasten off (see 3).

Left shoe Upper

Rnds 1–4: work as right shoe Upper

Rnd 5: ch1, 1sc in each of next 4[5] sts, ch3, skip next 5[6]sts (ch1 counts as stitch), 1sc in next sc, ch3, skip next 5[6]sts (ch1 counts as stitch), 1sc in each of next 5[6]sts. Continue with the strap, as folls: ch12[14], 1sc in 7th ch from hook, 1sc in each foll ch, sl st in next sc, 1sc in each of next 15[15]sts, join with sl st in ch1. Fasten off .

Weave in all ends. Sew a button on each shoe, for securing the strap.

cherry slippers

What's not to like about these cutesy, fruity slippers? A classic cream upper is trimmed in a bright green that creates two pretty leaf shapes at front of the shoe. The cherries are made separately and sewn on at the end.

Skill Level: I

Sizes
To fit ages:
0–6 months, sole length 3½in (9cm)
6–12 months, sole length 4in (10cm)
Changes for 6–12 months are in [ ]

Yarn

Main color (MC):
1oz (25g) DK-weight yarn
Shade: Cream
Contrasting colors (CC):
Small amounts DK-weight yarn
Shades: Bright green, red

Hooks & Notions
One size D (3.25mm) crochet hook or size needed to obtain gauge.
Tapestry needle

Gauge
10sts and 10 rows in sc to measure 2x2in (5x5cm)

Abbreviations
see page 134

Stitches & Skills
(see Crochet Basics, pages 133–141)
Special stitches used:
sc2tog
Techniques used:
Working in rounds
Working in front and back loops
Joining in yarn
Sole 1

The shoes
Both shoes are made in exactly the same way.
Sole
Make Sole 1 with MC.
Don't fasten off, but continue with the Upper.

Upper

With MC.

Rnd 1: working in back loops only ch1, 1sc in each of next 45[49]sts, join with sl st in first sc.

Rnds 2–4: working in both loops, repeat Rnd 1 (see 1).

Rnd 5: ch1, 1sc in each of next 4[6] sts, sc2tog 11[11] times, 1sc in each of next 19[21]sts, join with sl st in first sc (see 2).

Rnd 6: join in CC (green), ch1, 1sc in each of next 3[5]sts, ch5, skip next 6sts, 1sc in next st, ch5, skip next 6sts, sl st in next st (see 3).

Turn, ch5, skip ch5, 1sc in next sc, ch5, skip next ch5, sl st in next sc (see 4). Turn, ch5, skip next ch5, 1sc in next sc, ch5, skip next ch5, 1sc in same st as sl st, 1sc in each of next 17[19]sts, join with sl st in first sc. Fasten off.

Cherries

With CC (red); make four.

Foundation ring: ch3, join with sl st.

Rnd 1: ch1, 8sc into the ring, join with sl st in first sc. Fasten off, but leave a tail. Use tail to sew two cherries onto front of each slipper. Weave in all ends.

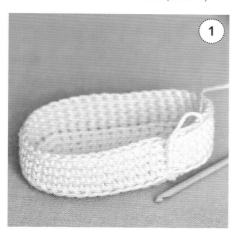

Skill Level: II

Sizes
To fit ages:
0–6 months, sole length 3½in (9cm)
6–12 months, sole length 4in (10cm)
Changes for 6–12 months are in [ ]

Yarn

Main color (MC):
1oz (25g) DK-weight yarn
Shade: Light gray
Contrasting color (CC):
Small amount DK-weight yarn
Shade: Dusky pink

Hooks & Notions
One size D (3.25mm) crochet hook
or size needed to obtain gauge
Tapestry needle

Gauge
10sts and 10 rows in sc to measure
2x2in (5x5cm)

Abbreviations
See page 134

Stitches & Skills
(see Crochet Basics, pages
133–141)
Special stitches used:
sc2tog
Techniques used:
Working in rows
Working in rounds
Working in front and back loops
Sole 1

rosebud party pumps

No party is complete without these elegant pumps. The pretty pink rose is worked flat and then shaped into its tight bud as it is sewn into place on the front of the shoe.

The shoes
Both shoes are made in exactly the same way.
Sole
Make Sole 1 with MC.
Don't fasten off, but continue with the Upper.

Upper

With MC.

Turn the Sole so that wrong side is facing you; working with the wrong side facing.

Rnd 1: working in the front loop only, ch1, 1sc in sl st of previous rnd (47[51]sc), 1sc in each foll st, join with sl st in first sc.

Rnd 2: working through both loops, ch1, skip st at base of ch-1, *1sc in next st, 1dc in next st; repeat from * 22[24] times more, join with sl st in first sc.

Rnd 3: ch1, 1sc in each next 46[50] sts, join with sl st in first sc.

Rnd 4: ch1, *1sc in next st, 1dc in next st; repeat from * 22[24] times more, join with sl st in first sc.

Rnd 5: ch1, 1sc in each of foll 22sts, sc2tog eight[ten] times, 1sc in each of next 8sts, join with sl st in first sc (see 1).

Rnd 6: ch1, *1sc in next st, 1dc in next st; repeat from * 18 [19] times more, join with sl st in first sc.

Rnd 7: ch1, 1sc in each of next 22[21]sts, sc2tog four[six] times,

> ## tip
> **Make sure that you work on the wrong side of the shoe once the Sole is complete. This is very important for the success of the pattern.**

1sc in each of next 8[7]sts, join with sl st in first sc.

Rnd 8: ch1, *1sc in next st, 1dc in next st; repeat from * 16 times more, join with sl st in first sc.

Turn shoe to the right side (see 2). Don't fasten off, but work straps as folls: ch25, 1sc in sl st in base of ch-25, 1sc in each of next 15sts across the Back, ch25, sl st in base of ch-25.
Fasten off (see 3).

Flower
With CC.
Foundation chain: ch20.
Row 1: 3dc in 4th ch from hook, *skip next ch, (1sc, ch2, 3dc) in next ch; repeat from * to last 2ch, skip next ch, 1sc in last ch.
Fasten off, but leave a tail (see 4). Thread the tail onto the tapestry needle. Starting with the last petal, and stitching as you go, coil the row of petals to give a flat base along the chain edge (see 5). Sew the flower onto the front of the shoe (see 6). Weave in all ends.

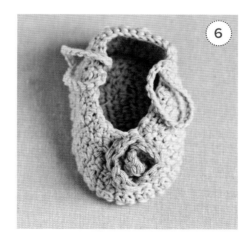

Sizes
To fit ages:
0–6 months, sole length 3½in (9cm)
6–12 months, sole length 4in (10cm)
Changes for 6–12 months are in [ ]

Yarn

2oz (50g) DK-weight yarn
Shade: Turquoise

Hooks & Notions
One size D (3.25mm) crochet hook
or size needed to obtain gauge
Four buttons

Gauge
10sts and 10 rows in sc to measure
2x2in (5x5cm)

Abbreviations
see page 134

Stitches & Skills
(see Crochet Basics, pages
133–141)
Special stitches used:
dc2tog
crab stitch
Techniques used:
Working in rows
Working in rounds
Joining in new yarn
Sole 1

molded clogs

Complete with the "riveted" ankle strap, these summer classics are a fun take on the molded plastic shoes that have become the last word in unisex footwear. Choose loud, bright colors for extra authenticity or make the strap in a contrasting color.

The shoes
Both shoes are made in exactly the same way.
Sole
Make Sole 1.
Fasten off.

Upper

Join yarn in st at center back of Sole heel.

Row 1: working in back loops only, ch3 (count as first dc), 1dc in each of next 45[49]sts, turn.

Row 2: working through both loops, ch1 (do not count as stitch), 1sc in base of ch-1, insert hook in same st and draw up a loop insert hook in next st and draw up a loop, draw last loop directly through 2 loops on hook, *insert hook in same st as last completed st, yarn over and draw up a loop, insert hook in next st and draw up a loop, draw last loop directly through two loops on hook; repeat from * to last st (45[49]sts), sl st in 3rd ch of ch-3 of Row 1, turn.

Row 3: ch3 (count as first dc), working in back loops only, skip sl st, 1dc in each of next 10[12] sts, dc2tog 12 times, 1dc in each of next 11[13]sts, turn (see 1).

Row 4: working through both loops, ch1 (do not count as stitch), 1sc in base of ch-1, insert hook in same st and draw up a loop, insert hook in next st and draw up a loop, draw last loop directly through two loops on hook, *insert hook in same st as last completed st, yarn over and draw up a loop, insert hook in next st and draw up a loop, draw last loop directly through two loops on hook; repeat from * to last st (33[37]sts), sl st in 3rd ch of ch-3 of Row 3, turn.

Row 5: working in back loops only, ch3 (count as first dc), skip sl st, 1dc in each of next 7[9]sts, *skip 2sts, 1dc in next st; repeat from * five times more, 1dc in each of next 8[10]sts (see 2).

Turn shoe inside out and join heel seam, working sl st across. Fasten off. Turn shoe to the right side.

Edging

Join yarn in st at center back of shoe.

Rnd 1: ch1, and work crab stitch in each st, join with sl st in first sc. Fasten off. (see 3).

Strap

Foundation chain: ch25[27].

Row 1: 1sc in 2nd ch from hook, 1sc in each foll ch (24[26]sc), turn.

Row 2: ch1 (do not count as st), 1sc in first st, insert hook in same st and draw up a loop, insert hook in next st and draw up a loop, draw last loop directly through two loops on hook, *insert hook in same st as last completed st, yarn over and draw up a loop, insert hook in next st and draw up a loop, draw last loop directly through two loops on hook; repeat from * to end (24[26]sts), turn.

Row 3: working in back loops only, ch1, 1sc in each of next 24[26]sts. Fasten off (see 4).

Weave in all ends.

For each shoe, position one button on one end of the strap and sew it to one side of the shoe. Position a second button on the opposite end of the strap and sew it to the other side of the shoe.

tip

Take care with Row 2 of both the Upper and the strap. You need to draw the last loop directly through two loops on the hook. You don't want to yarn over and then draw the last loop through all the loops you have on the hook.

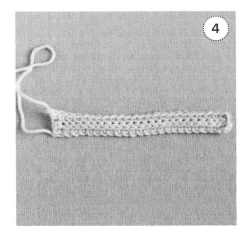

Skill Level: III

Sizes

To fit ages:
0–6 months, sole length 3½in (9cm)
6–12 months, sole length 4in (10cm)
Changes for 6–12 months are in [ ]

Yarn

Main color (MC)
2oz (50g) DK-weight yarn
Shade: Tan
Contrasting color (CC)
Small amount 4-ply yarn
Shade: Cream

Hooks & Notions

One size D (3.25mm) crochet hook
or size needed to obtain gauge

Gauge

10sts and 10 rows in sc to measure
2x2in (5x5cm)

Abbreviations

See page 134

Stitches & Skills

(see Crochet Basics, pages
133–141)
Special stitches used:
dc2tog
Techniques used:
Working in rows
Working in rounds
Working in front and back loops
Working in remaining loop
Joining in yarn
Sole 1
Twisted cord

moccasins

If it's comfort you're after, you need look no further than this pair of moccasins—the perfect choice for lounging around in pjs. This design comes with all the trimmings: contrasting laces and soft, fringed edging.

The shoes

Both shoes are made in exactly the same way.
Sole
Make Sole 1 with MC.
Don't fasten off, but continue with Upper.

Upper

With MC.

Rnd 1: working in back loops only, ch1, 1sc in each of next 45[49]sc, join with sl st in first sc.

Rnds 2–4: working in both loops, repeat Rnd 1.

Rnd 5: working in both loops, ch1, 1sc in each of next 5[6]sts, working in back loops only, dc2tog nine[ten] times, working in both loops, 1sc in each of next 22[23] sts, join with sl st in first sc (see 1).

Rnd 6: ch1, 1sc in each of next 3[4] sts, skip next 2sts, 1dc in each of next 9[10]sts, skip next 2sts, 1sc in each of next 20[21]sts, join with sl st in first sc, work sl st in each of next 3[4]sts, turn. Continue with the Back working in rows (see 2).

Back

With MC.

Row 1: ch1, 1sc in each of next 4[5]sl sts, 1sc in each of next 19[20]sts, turn.

Row 2: ch1, 1sc in each of next 23[25]sts, turn.

Rows 3–8: repeat Row 2.

Row 9: *ch6, sl st in next st; repeat from * to end, turn (see 3). Fold Back down, so that Row 8 meets Row 1, working through sts of Row 8 and Row 1, sl st in each st to join (see 4).

Tongue
With MC. Work in 9[10]dc of the Front.
Row 1: ch1, 1sc in st at base of ch-1, 1sc in each of next 8[9]sts, turn (see 5).
Row 2: ch1, 1sc in each of next 9[10]sts, turn.
Rows 3–5: repeat Row 2.

Row 6: ch1, skip next sc, 1sc in each of next 6[7]sts, skip next st, 1sc in last st. Fasten off (see 6).

Edging
With MC. With right side facing, join yarn to right-hand side of remaining loops of Rnd 5 of Upper, sl st in each loop. Fasten off (see 7). Weave in all ends. Make a twisted cord measuring 19½in (50cm) with CC. Use crochet hook to thread cord through edging at top of shoe (see 8).

super cute boots

A fine collection of colorful booties that babies will love to kick around in. Styles cater to the tastes and needs of modern-day girls and boys, and you'll find something for every occasion: baseball boots for the sporty type; vintage bow boots for party elegance; and heavy-duty work boots for those times when a dude just has to get the job done!

Sizes
To fit ages:
0–6 months, sole length 3½in (9cm)
6–12 months, sole length 4in (10cm)
Changes for 6–12 months are in [ ]

Yarn

Main color (MC):
2oz (50g) DK-weight yarn
Shade: Dusky pink
Contrasting color (CC):
1oz (25g) DK-weight yarn
Shade: White

Hooks & Notions
One size D (3.25mm) crochet hook
or size needed to obtain gauge
Tapestry needle

Gauge
10sts and 10 rows in sc to measure
2x2in (5x5cm)

Abbreviations
see page 134

Stitches & Skills
(see Crochet Basics, pages
133–141)
Special stitches used:
sc2tog
Techniques used:
Working in rows
Working in rounds
Working in front and back loops
Sole 1

vintage bow boots

The sweetest "first-ever" pair of boots, with fine, lace-effect ankles and a contrasting bow to the side. These pretty booties lend a certain Victorian elegance to any outfit.

The boots
Both boots are made in exactly the same way.
Sole
Make Sole 1 with MC.
Don't fasten off, but continue with Upper.

Upper

With MC. Working in back loops only (Rnds 1–10).

Rnd 1: ch1, skip st at base of ch-1, 1sc in each of next 45[49]sts, join with sl st in first sc.

Rnds 2–3: repeat Rnd 1 (see 1).

Rnd 4: ch1, 1sc in each of next 6sts, *skip next st, 1sc in next st; repeat from * eight[ten] times more, 1sc in each of next 21sts, join with sl st in first sc.

Rnd 5: ch1, 1sc in each of next 4sts, *skip next st, 1sc in next st; repeat from * five[six] times more, 1sc in each of next 20sts, join with sl st in first sc.

Rnd 6: ch1, 1sc in each of next 30[31]sts, join with sl st in first sc.

Rnd 7: ch1, 1sc in each of next 3sts, *skip next st, 1sc in next st; repeat from * four[four] times more, 1sc in each of next 17[18]sts, join with sl st in first sc.

Rnd 8: ch1, 1sc in each of next 25[26]sts, join with sl st in first sc.

Rnds 9–10: repeat Rnd 8 (see 2).

Working in both loops:

Rnd 11: ch3 (count as first dc), 1dc in next st, *skip next st, ch1, 1dc in each of next 2sts; repeat from * seven times more, ch1, join with sl st in 3rd ch of ch-3. For 6–12 months, skip last st.

Rnd 12: ch5, skip next dc, 1dc in next ch-1 space, *ch2, skip next 2dc, 1dc in next ch-1 space; repeat from * seven times more, join with sl st in 3rd ch of ch-5.

Rnd 13: ch1, *5dc in each of next ch-2 space, skip next dc, 1sc in next ch-2 space; repeat from * four times more, but in last repeat instead of sc work sl st in sl st of previous Rnd. Fasten off (see 3).

Bow

With CC.

Row 1: ch3, 1sc in second ch from hook, 1sc in next ch, turn.

Row 2: ch1, 2sc in each of next 2sts, turn.

Row 3: ch1, 1sc in each of next 4sts, turn.

Rows 4–11: repeat Row 3 eight times more.

Row 12: ch1, sc2tog twice, turn.

Row 13: ch1, 2sc in each of next 2sts, turn.

Rows 14–22: repeat Row 3 nine times more.

Row 23: ch1, sc2tog twice.

Put both ends together and join with sl sts.

Fasten off leaving a long tail.

Bow tail

With CC.

Row 1: ch4, 1sc in 2nd ch, 1 sc in each foll ch, turn.

Row 2: ch1, 1sc in each of next 3sts, turn.

Rows 3–5: repeat Row 2 three times more.

Row 6: ch3 (count as first dc), skip next st, 1dc in last st, turn.

Row 7: ch1, 2sc in next st, 1sc in next st, turn.

Rows 8–11: repeat Row 2 four times more. Fasten off (see 4).

tip

These elegant boots work equally well in blue, purple, and green. You can make the side bows in a slightly smaller size if you like. Simply use a lighter weight yarn and smaller crochet hook.

Press bow so that seam is exactly in the middle, place it on bow tail and wrap tail of yarn around both pieces few times. Thread tapestry needle with remaining length of tail and sew one bow onto the external side of each bootie. Weave in all ends.

Sizes

To fit ages:
0–6 months, sole length 3½in (9cm)
6–12 months, sole length 4in (10cm)
Changes for 6–12 months are in [ ]

Yarn

2oz (50g) DK-weight yarn
Shade: Light blue

Hooks & Notions

One size D (3.25mm) crochet hook
or size needed to obtain gauge
Four buttons
Tapestry needle

Gauge

10sts and 10 rows in sc to measure
2x2in (5x5cm)

Abbreviations

See page 134

Stitches & Skills

(see Crochet Basics, pages
133–141)
Special stitches used:
sc2tog
dc8tog
Techniques used:
Working in rows
Working in rounds
Working in front and back loops
Sole 1

button boots

A pair of supercute booties for all babies. Best suited to pastel shades with contrasting buttons, they have a simple wrapover flap at the ankle, making them adjustable for a snug fit.

The boots

Follow separate instructions for right and left straps.
Sole
Make Sole 1.
Don't fasten off, but continue with Upper.

Upper

Rnd 1: working in back loops only, ch1, sl st at base of ch-1, 1sc in each of next 45[49]sts, join with sl st in first sc.

Rnds 2–4: working in both loops, repeat Rnd 1 (see 1).

Rnd 5: ch1, 1sc in each of next 3[5] sts, *sc2tog, 1sc in next st; repeat from * seven times more, 1sc in each of next 18[20]sts, join with sl st in first sc.

Rnd 6: ch1, 1sc in each of next 3[5] sts, sc2tog eight times, 1sc in each of next 18[20]sts, join with sl st in first sc (see 2).

Rnd 7: ch1, 1sc in each of next 3[5] sts, dc8tog, 1sc in each of next 18[20]sts, join with sl st in first sc (see 3). Don't fasten off but work strap in rows as folls:

Right bootie: Row 1: ch16[17], turn, 1dc in 4th ch from hook (count as first dc), 1dc in each of foll ch, work 1dc in each of next 24[28] sts around Upper toward the Heel and back toward the beg-ch,

tip

These boots look great if worked in two (or more) colors. Change the yarn in each round to create a beautiful striped effect.

(including sl st of previous Rnd), turn (see 4).

Left bootie: Fasten off. Join in yarn in the 9th[13th]sts along the Upper from the first sc st.

Row 1: ch16[17], turn, 1dc in 4th ch from hook (count as first dc), 1dc in each foll ch, 1dc in same st as last sl st, work 1dc in each of next 23[27]sts, around Upper, toward the Heel and back toward the beg-ch, turn (see 5).

Both booties: Row 2: ch3 (counts as first dc), 1dc in each of next 37[42]sts (last dc always work in 3rd ch of ch-3) (38[43]dc), turn.

Rows 3–6: repeat Row 2 (see 6). Work ch1, sc evenly across strap edge as shown (see 7). Fasten off.

Weave in all ends. Sew two buttons onto each bootie for fastening the straps. There are no special holes for the buttons, but you can use spaces between dc stitches for this. This will make it easier to adjust the ankle strap for a better fit.

Sizes

To fit ages:
0–6 months, sole length 3½in (9cm)
6–12 months, sole length 4in (10cm)
Changes for 6–12 months are in [ ]

Yarn

Main color (MC):
2oz (50g) DK-weight yarn
Shade: Tan
Contrasting colors (CC):
Small amounts DK-weight yarn
Shades: Dark brown, silver

Hooks & Notions

One size D (3.25mm) crochet hook
or size needed to obtain gauge
Tapestry needle

Gauge

10sts and 10 rows in sc to measure
2x2in (5x5cm)

Abbreviations

see page 134

Stitches & Skills

(see Crochet Basics, pages
133–141)
Special stitches used:
dc2tog
crab stitch
Techniques used:
Working in rounds
Working in front and back loops
Sole 1

cowboy boots

This neat little pair of ankle-high booties comes complete with side straps, chain, and spurs—just the ticket for heading to a hoedown. Opt for an authentic leather color—black, dark brown, or as here, tan.

The boots

Both boots are made in exactly the same way.
Sole
Make Sole 1 with MC.
Don't fasten off, but continue with Upper.

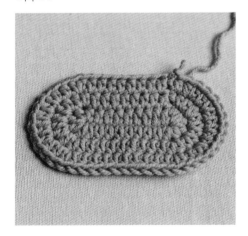

Upper

Rnd 1: working in back loops only, ch1, 1sc in each of next 46[50]sts, join with sl st in first sc.

Rnd 2: working in both loops, ch3 (count as first dc), 1dc in each of next 5[6]sts, dc2tog nine[ten] times, 1dc in next 23[24]sts, join with sl st in 3rd ch of ch-3 (see 1).

Rnd 3: ch1, 1sc in each of next 37[40]sts, join with sl st in first sc.

Rnd 4: ch3 (count as first dc), 1dc in each of next 3[4]sts, dc2tog seven[eight] times, 1dc in each of next 20[20]sts, join with sl st in 3rd ch of ch-3.

Rnd 5: ch1, 1sc in each of next 30[32]sts, join with sl st in first sc (see 2).

Rnd 6: ch3 (count as first dc), 1dc in each of next 30[32]sts, join with sl st in 3rd ch of ch-3.

Rnd 7: repeat Rnd 6.

Rnd 8: ch3 (count as first dc), 1dc in each of next 3[3]sts, 1sc in each of next 8[9]sts, 1dc in each of next 7[7]sts, 1sc in each of next 9[10] sts, 1dc in each of next 3[3]sts, join

with sl st in 3rd ch of ch-3 (see 3).
Rnd 9: ch1, 1sc in each of next 3[3] sts, sl st in each of next 8[9]sts, 1sc in each of next 7[7]sts, sl st in each of next 9[10]sts, 1sc in each of next 3[3]sts, join with sl st in first sc. Fasten off.

Strap
With MC.
Foundation chain: ch15.
Rnd 1: 1sc in 2nd ch from hook, 1sc in each of foll 12ch, (3dc, ch1, 3dc) in last ch, rotate work, working along opposite edge into remaining loop, 1sc in each of next 13sts. Fasten off (see 4). Sew strap onto outside edge of boot (see 5).

Spur
With CC (silver).
Foundation ring: ch4, join with sl st in first ch.
Rnd 1: ch1, 6sc into ring, join with sl st in first sc.
Rnd 2: *ch4, sl st in 3rd ch from hook, ch1, sl st in next sc* repeat from * six times more, working the

last sl st of the last repeat into the base of the first ch-4. Fasten off (see 6).

Chain

With CC (silver).
Foundation chain: ch15.
Row 1: sl st in 2nd ch from hook, *ch1, skip 1ch, sl st in next ch*; repeat from * to end. Fasten off. Pass chain through the Foundation ring of the Spur (see 7). Sew both ends onto back of boot (see 8).

Heel

With CC (dark brown). Working in remaining loops of the Sole, join yarn in 4th stitch from the joining line, work evenly sc around (see 9). Join with sl st in first sc (see 10) Don't turn. Work crab stitch (see 11) , until the corresponding stitch on the opposite side of the Sole is reached. Fasten off (see 12). Weave in all ends.

Sizes

To fit ages:
0–6 months, sole length 3½in (8.5cm)
6–12 months, sole length 3¾in (9.5cm)

Yarn

Main color (MC):
1 oz (25g) DK-weight yarn
Shade: Brown
Contrasting color (CC):
1oz (25g) DK-weight yarn
Shade: Cream

Hooks & Notions

One size D (3.25mm) crochet hook or size needed to obtain gauge

Gauge

10sts and 10 rows in sc to measure 2x2in (5x5cm)

Abbreviations

See page 134

Stitches & Skills

(see Crochet Basics, pages 133–141)
Special stitches used:
dc2tog
Techniques used:
Working in rounds
Working in front and back loops
Joining in yarn
Sole 1

furry boots

This super-cozy pair of fluffy "fur" boots makes trekking out on chilly winter days a breeze. Each round of the fleecy trim is made by working a round of single-crochet into a round of loops.

The boots

Both boots are made in exactly the same way.
Sole
Make Sole 1 with MC.
Don't fasten off, but continue with Upper.

Upper

With MC.

Rnd 1: working in back loops only, ch1, skip st at base of ch-1, 1sc in each of next 45[49]sts, join with sl st in first sc.

6–12 months: Decrease rnd: working in both loops, ch1, 1sc in each of next 11sts, skip next 2sts, 1dc in each of next 9sts, skip next 2sts, 1sc in each of next 25sts, join with sl st in first sc.

Both sizes: working in both loops.

Rnd 2: ch1, 1sc in each of next 9sts, skip next 2sts, 1dc in each of next 9sts, skip next 2sts, 1sc in each of next 23sts, join with sl st in first sc.

Rnd 3: ch1, 1sc in each of next 7sts, skip next 2sts, 1dc in each of next 9sts, skip next 2sts, 1sc in each of next 21sts, join with sl st in first sc.

Rnd 4: ch1, 1sc in each of next 5sts, skip next 2sts, 1dc in each of next 9sts, skip next 2sts, 1sc in each of next 19sts, join with sl st in first sc.

Rnd 5: ch1, 1sc in each of next 3sts, skip next 2sts, 1dc in each of next 9sts, skip next 2sts, 1sc in each of next 17sts, join with sl st in first sc.

Rnd 6: ch3, 1dc in each of next 3sts, dc2tog five times, 1dc in each of next 16sts, join with sl st in 3rd ch of ch-3 (see 1).

Rnd 7: join in CC, *ch6, sl st into front loop of next st; repeat from * to end, do not join, (see 2).
(24 loops made)

Rnd 8: ch1, 1sc into back loop of next 24sts on Rnd 6, join with sl st in first sc (see 3).

Rnds 9–18: repeat Rnds 7 and 8 five times more. Fasten off.

Sizes
To fit ages:
0–6 months, sole length 3½in (9cm)
6–12 months, sole length 4in (10cm)
Changes for 6–12 months are in [ ]

Yarn

Main color (MC):
2oz (50g) Aran-weight yarn
Shade: Chalk white
Contrasting color (CC):
Small amount DK-weight yarn
Shade: Gray

Hooks & Notions
One size E (3.5mm) crochet hook
or size needed to obtain gauge

Gauge
9sts and 9 rows in sc to measure
2x2in (5x5cm)

Abbreviations
see page 134

Stitches & Skills
(see Crochet Basics, pages
133–141)
Special stitches used:
sc2tog
dc2tog
Techniques used:
Working in rows
Working in rounds
Working in front and back loops
Joining in yarn
Sole 2
Twisted cord

desert boots

A sleek pair of desert boots for that sophisticated, smart-casual look. Perfect paired with jeans, everyday pants, and shorts, these neutral-colored boots are a must-have wardrobe staple.

The boots
Both boots are made in exactly the same way.
Sole
Make Sole 2 with MC.
Don't fasten off, but continue with Upper.

Upper

With MC. Work with wrong side facing. Note: ch1 doesn't count as stitch.

Rnd 1: working in front loops only, ch1, skip sl st, *1sc in next st, 1hdc in next st; repeat from * to end (42[46]sts), join with sl st in first sc. Working in both loops:

Rnd 2: ch1, *1hdc in next st, 1sc in next st; repeat from * to end (42[46]sts), join with sl st in first sc.

Rnd 3: ch1, *1sc in next st, 1hdc in next st; repeat from * to end (42[46]sts), join with sl st in first sc (see 1).

Rnd 4: ch1, (1hdc in next st, 1sc in next st) nine times, *skip next st, 1sc in next st; repeat from * eight[ten] times more, repeat again from (1hdc in next st, 1sc in next st) twice, join with sl st in first sc.

Turn bootie so right side is facing. Continue working towards the Front.

Rnd 5: ch1, skip sl st, 1sc in each of next 3sts, skip next 2sts, dc2tog

tip

To make these boots taller, repeat Rows 1 and 2 of the Ankle twice (instead of once) and repeat Row 2 of the tongue six times (instead of four). Make an extra loop on each side for the lace.

four[five] times, skip next 2sts, 1sc in each of next 18sts, join with sl st in first sc, sl st in each of next 3sts (see 2).

Don't fasten off, turn, continue with Ankle.

Ankle

With MC. For both sizes. Working in rows.

Row 1: ch1, *1hdc in next st, 1sc in next st; repeat from * ten times more across the Back, turn (see 3).

Row 2: ch1, 1sc in each of next 22sts, turn.

Rows 3–4: repeat Rows 1 and 2 once more. Do not turn at the end of Row 4.

Work loops for lace along side of ankle part as folls:

Row 5: *ch3, skip next row, sl st in next row; repeat from * twice more. Fasten off. Join the yarn in first st on opposite side of ankle part and repeat (see 4).

Tongue

With MC.

Row 1: ch1, 2sc in each st across the Toe, (8[10]sc) turn.

Row 2: ch1, 1sc in each of next 8[10]sts, turn.

Rows 3–6: repeat Row 2 four times more.

Row 7: ch1, sc2tog, 1sc in each of next 4[6]sts, sc2tog.

Fasten off (see 5).

Weave in all ends.

Make a twisted cord measuring 19½in (50cm) with CC. Lace up front of the boot using loops made on side of Ankle. Tie a bow.

3). Fasten off and turn the bootie to right side.

Tongue
With CC. For both sizes. Join yarn to st right-hand side of Toe edge.
Row 1: ch1, 7sc evenly across the center of Toe, turn.
Rows 2–6: ch1, 1sc in each of next 7sts, turn.
Row 7: ch1, sc2tog, 1sc in each of next 3sts, sc2tog, turn.
Rows 8–9: ch1, 1sc in each of next 5sts, turn. Fasten off (see 4).

Edging
With MC. Join yarn to st on the right-hand side of Toe edge.
Row 1: 1ch, work sc evenly across Toe and tongue, do not turn.
Row 2: work crab st in each st. Fasten off (see 5).

Upper
With MC. Join yarn to 4th front loop from right-hand edge of Toe Row 1 (see 6).
Row 1: ch1, 1sc in st at base of ch-1, 1sc in each of next 29[28] sts (work in remaining loops, but where you have two loops work in both), turn.
Row 2: ch1, 1sc in each of next 30[29]sts, turn.
Row 3: ch1, sc2tog, ch1, skip next st, 1sc in each of next 24[23]sts, ch1, skip next st, sc2tog, turn.
Row 4: ch1, 1sc in each of next 28[27]sts and ch-1 spaces, turn.
Row 5: ch1, sc2tog, ch1, skip next st, 1sc in each of next 22[21]sts, ch1, skip next st, sc2tog, turn.

Row 6: ch1, 1sc in each of next 26[25]sts and ch-1 spaces, turn.
Row 7: ch1, 1sc in next st, ch1, skip next st, 1sc in each of next 22[21] sts, ch1, skip next st, 1sc in next stitch, turn.
Rows 8–9: repeat Rows 6–7.
Row 10: repeat Row 6.
Fasten off (see 7).

Edging
With CC. Join yarn to first st of Upper.
Row 1: ch1, work 1sc evenly across row ends, along last row of Upper, 1sc evenly across row ends, don't turn.
Row 2: work crab st in each st. Fasten off (see 8).

Stripes
With CC. Using the photograph as reference, join in yarn at the base of one of the diagonal stripes. Working in sl st, work a diagonal line of stitches. (see 9).

Weave in all ends. Make a twisted cord measuring 25in (65cm) with CC and lace up both sides of the boot.

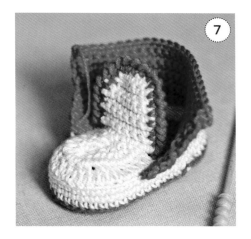

biker boots

Get that motor running! Complete with adjustable straps, these neat little boots epitomize the heavy leather look of their classic inspiration. Make them in black or dark brown for the last word in biker chic!

Sizes
To fit ages:
0–6 months, sole length 3½in (9cm)
6–12 months, sole length 4in (10cm)
Changes for 6–12 months are in [ ]

Yarn

2oz (50g) DK-weight yarn
Shade: Dark brown

Hooks & Notions
One size D (3.25mm) crochet hook
or size needed to obtain gauge
Four buttons
Tapestry needle

Gauge
10sts and 10 rows in sc to measure
2x2in (5x5cm)

Abbreviations
see page 134

Stitches & Skills
(see Crochet Basics, pages
133–141)
Special stitches used:
FP dc
BP dc
dc2tog
Techniques used:
Working in rounds
Joining in yarn
Double Sole 1

The boots
Follow separate instructions for
making right and left boots.
Sole
Make Double Sole 1.
Fasten off.

Upper

Join yarn into the center stitch of the Sole Heel.

Working in sl sts worked to join the Soles, continue as folls:

Rnd 1: ch3 (count as first dc) 1dc in each of next 45[49]sts, join with sl st on 3rd ch of ch-3.

Rnd 2: ch3, *1FP dc around next st, 1BP dc around next st; repeat from * 21[23] times more, 1FP dc around next st, join with sl st in 3rd ch of ch-3 (see 1).

Next round (6–12 months only):

ch1, 1sc in each of next 17sts, skip next 2sts, 1dc in each of next 11sts, skip next 2sts, 1sc in each of next 17sts, join with sl st in first sc.

Both sizes note: round count continues as for 0–6 months—add 1 round to count for 6–12 months.

Rnd 3: ch1, skip st at base of ch-1, 1sc in each of next 15sts, skip next 2sts, 1dc in each of next 11sts, skip next 2sts, 1sc in each of next 15sts, join with sl st in first sc.

Rnd 4: ch1, 1sc in each of next 13sts, skip next 2sts, 1dc in each of next 11sts, skip next 2sts, 1sc in each of next 13sts, join with sl st in first sc.

Rnd 5: ch1, 1sc in next 11sts, skip next 2sts, dc2tog five times, 1dc in next st, skip next 2sts, 1sc in each of next 11sts, join with sl st in first sc (see 2).

Rnd 6: ch1, 1sc in each of next 28sts, join with sl st in first sc.

Rnds 7–16: repeat Rnd 6 ten times more (see 3). Do not fasten off.

Right bootie

Next Rnd: ch1, 1sc in each of next 22sts, 5dc in next st, 1sc in each of next 5sts, join with sl st in first sc.

Next Rnd: ch1, 1sc in each of next 22sts, *1FP dc around next dc, 1BP dc around next dc; repeat from * once more, 1FP dc around next dc, 1sc in each of next 5sts, join with sl st in first sc.

Next Rnd: repeat previous Rnd. Fasten off (see 4).

Left bootie

Next Rnd: ch1, 1sc in each of next 6sts, 5dc in next st, 1sc in each of next 21sts, join with sl st in first sc.

Next Rnd: ch1, 1sc in each of next 6sts, *1FP dc around next dc, 1BP dc around next dc; repeat from * once more, 1FP dc around next dc, 1sc in each of next 21sts, join with sl st in first sc.

Next Rnd: repeat previous Rnd. Fasten off.

Strap

Make two for each boot.
Foundation chain: ch10.

Rnd 1: 1sc in 2nd ch from hook, 1sc in each of foll 7ch, 5sc in last ch, rotate work, working along the opposite edge into remaining loop, 1sc in each of next 7sts, 4sc in last st, join with sl st in first sc. Fasten off.

Using the photograph as reference, sew two straps to each boot. The buttons should be always on external side of the bootie (see 5).
Position first strap across front of bootie, at Ankle. Sew one end of strap to side of bootie. Place a button on opposite end of strap and sew both to side of the bootie. Position second strap on side of bootie, at 5dc and stitch end at front of boot in place. Place a button on opposite end of strap and sew both to other side of 5dc. Weave in all ends.

Skill Level: III

Sizes
To fit ages:
0–6 months, sole length 3½in (9cm)
6–12 months, sole length 4in (10cm)
Changes for 6–12 months are in [ ]

Yarn

Main color (MC):
2oz (50g) DK-weight yarn
Shade: Bright blue
Contrasting color (CC):
Small amount DK-weight yarn
Shade: Gray

Hooks & Notions
One size D (3.25mm) crochet hook
or size needed to obtain gauge
Stitch marker

Gauge
10sts and 10 rows in sc to measure
2x2in (5x5cm)

Abbreviations
See page 134

Stitches & Skills
(see Crochet Basics, pages
133–141)
Special stitches used:
FP dc
BP dc
Techniques used:
Working in rounds
Working in front and back loops
Working in remaining loop
Joining in yarn
Sole 1
Twisted cord

snow boots

Cool snow boots in bright aqua yarn—sure to lighten the mood on gray, snowy days. These booties are finished with "rubber" soles to the base and drawstring ties at the top for keeping all that lovely warmth in.

The boots
Both boots are made in exactly the same way.
Sole
Make Sole 1 with MC.
Don't fasten off, but continue with Upper.

Upper

Change to CC, but do not cut MC.

Rnd 1: working in back loops only ch1, skip st at base of ch-1, 1sc in each of next 2sts, working in both loops, 1sc in each of next 26[30] sts, working in back loops only, 1sc in each of next 17sts, (45[49]sc), join with sl st in first sc. Break off CC, continue with MC.

Rnd 2: ch1, 2sc in next st, (skip next st, 2sc in next st) to end (46[50]sc), join with sl st in first sc (see 1).

Rnd 3: ch1, 2sc in next st, (skip next st, 2sc in next st) to last st, (46[50]sc), skip last st, join with sl st in first sc.

Rnd 4: ch1, 2sc in next st, (skip next st, 2sc in next st) three times, *skip next st, 1sc in next st; repeat from *seven[nine] times more, (skip next st, 2sc in next st) 11 times more, skip last st, (38[40]sc), join with sl st in first sc (see 2).

Rnd 5: ch1, 2sc in next st, (skip next st, 2sc in next st) to last st, skip last st, join with sl st in first sc (38[40]sc).

Rnd 6: ch1, 2sc in next st, (skip next st, 2sc in next st) three times, *skip next st, 1sc in next st; repeat from * five[seven] times more, (skip next st, 2sc in next st) nine[eight] times more, skip last st, (32[32]sc) don't join but work next Rnd.

Working in a spiral:

Rnds 7–14: skip ch1, place stitch marker in ch-1, (2sc in next sc, skip next sc) repeat until eight rounds are

completed, sl st in next st
(see 3).

Rnd 15: ch3, 1dc in each of next 32sts, join with sl st in 3rd ch of ch-3.

Rnd 16: ch3, *1FP dc around next st, 1BP dc around next st; repeat from * to end, join with sl st in 3rd ch of ch-3 (see 4). Fasten off.

Heel

With CC. With the right side facing join yarn to the right-hand side of the remaining loops of Rnd

1 of Upper, (see 5), working in remaining loops, ch1, 1sc in st at base of ch-1, 1sc in each of next 19sts, do not turn, work crab stitch in each st (see 6).
Fasten off (see 7).

Weave in all ends. Make a twisted cord, measuring 17¾in (45cm) with CC. Starting from the front of the boot, weave the cord through the stitches of the last round.
Tie a bow.

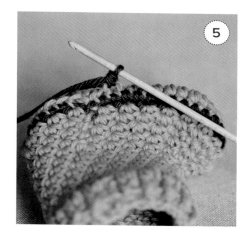

Skill Level: III

Sizes

To fit ages:
0–6 months, sole length 3½in (9cm)
6–12 months, sole length 4in (10cm)
Changes for 6–12 months are in [ ]

Yarn

Main color (MC):
2oz (50g) DK-weight yarn
Shade: Orange
Contrasting color (CC):
Small amount DK-weight yarn
Shade: Dark brown

Hooks & Notions

One size D (3.25mm) crochet hook
or size needed to obtain gauge

Gauge

10sts and 10 rows in sc to measure
2x2in (5x5cm)

Abbreviations

see page 134

Stitches & Skills

(see Crochet Basics, pages
133–141)
Special stitches used:
FP dc
BP dc
Techniques used:
Working in rounds
Working in front and back loops
Working in remaining loop
Joining in yarn
Sole 1
Twisted cord

work boots

This extra-tall pair of heavy-duty work boots is just perfect for the dude who's into diggers and trucks. There are six pairs of holes on each boot, so be sure to make double length twisted cords for the laces.

The boots

Both boots are made in exactly the same way.
Sole
Make Sole 1 with MC.
Don't fasten off, but continue with the Upper.

Upper

With MC.

Rnd 1: working in back loops only ch1, 1sc in each of next 46[50]sts, join with sl st in first sc.

Rnd 2: working in both loops ch1, 1sc in each of next 9[11]sts, skip next 2sts, 1dc in each of next 9sts, skip 2sts, 1sc in each of next 24[26]sts, join with sl st in first sc.

Rnd 3: ch1, 1sc in each of next 7[9] sts, skip 2sts, *1FP dc around next st, 1BP dc around next st; repeat from * three times more, 1FP dc around next st, skip 2sts, 1sc in each of next 22[24]sts, join with sl st in first sc (see 1).

Rnd 4: ch1, 1sc in each of next 5[7]sts, skip next 2sts, *1FP dc around next st, 1BP dc around next st; repeat from * three times more, 1FP dc around next st, skip 2sts, 1sc in each of next 20[22]sts, join with sl st in first sc.

Rnd 5: ch1, 1sc in each of next 3[5]sts, skip next 2sts, *1FP dc around next st, 1BP dc around next st; repeat from * three times more, 1FP dc around next st, skip 2sts, 1sc in each of next

18[20]sts, join with sl st in first sc.

Rnd 6: ch1, 1sc in each of next 1[3]sts, skip next 2sts, *1FP dc around next st, 1BP dc around next st; repeat from * three times more, 1FP dc around next st, skip 2sts, 1sc in each of next 16[18]sts, join with sl st in first sc (see 2).

For size 6–12 months only:

Rnd 7: ch1, 1sc in next st, skip next 2sts, *1FP dc around next st, 1BP dc around next st; repeat from * three times more, 1FP dc around next st, skip 2sts, 1sc in each of next 16sts, join with sl st in first sc.

Ankle

With MC.

Rnd 1: ch3, 1dc in next st, *1FP dc around next st, 1BP dc around next st; repeat from * three times more, 1FP dc around next st, 1dc in each of next 16sts, join with sl st in 3rd ch of ch-3.

Rnd 2: ch3, 1BP dc around next st, *1FP dc around next st, 1BP dc around next st; repeat from * three times more, 1FP dc around next st, **1BP dc around next 2sts, 1FP dc around next

2sts; repeat from ** three times more, join with sl st in 3rd ch of ch-3.

Rnd 3: repeat Rnd 2.

Rnd 4: ch3, 1FP dc around next st, *1FP dc around next st, 1BP dc around next st; repeat from * three times more, 1FP dc around next st, **1FP dc around next 2sts, 1BP dc around next 2sts; repeat from ** three times more, join with sl st in 3rd ch of ch-3.

Rnd 5: repeat Rnd 4.

Rnds 6–7: repeat Rnd 2 twice more. Fasten off (see 3).

Weave in all ends. Make two twisted cords measuring 29½in (75cm) with CC. Lace up front of boot, passing cord through first and last FP dc of Front. Tie a bow. (see 4).

tip

Instead of making a twisted cord, crochet a length of chain until you have enough to lace up the two sides of one boot. Then repeat to make another lace for the second boot.

super cute sandals

Liven up your baby's summer wardrobe with a pair of super cute sandals. With styles to suit all girls and boys, designs range from classic sandals for pure comfort, through Grecian and gladiator models, to glam pairs with pompoms, bows, and flowers. Summer will never be the same again!

Sizes
To fit ages:
0–6 months, sole length 3½in (9cm)
6–12 months, sole length 4in (10cm)
Changes for 6–12 months are in [ ]

Yarn

1oz (25g) DK-weight yarn
Shade: Yellow

Hooks & Notions
One size D (3.25mm) crochet hook
or size needed to obtain gauge
Tapestry needle
Two buttons

Gauge
10sts and 10 rows in sc to measure
2x2in (5x5cm)

Abbreviations
see page 134

Stitches & Skills
(see Crochet Basics, pages
133–141)
Special stitches used:
sc2tog
Techniques used:
Working in rows
Working in rounds
Joining in new yarn
Double Sole 1

jelly sandals

What better way to spend long
summer days than sporting a pair of
jolly jelly sandals in a pastel shade?
This is a simple design that involves
working three straps across the toe
section of the sandal.

The sandals
Follow separate instructions for right
and left sandals.
Sole
Make a Double Sole 1.
Fasten off.

Back right sandal

Join yarn in central st of 9[11]hdc on the side of the Sole. Working in both loops of sl sts used to join the Soles.

Row 1: ch1, 1sc in the base of ch-1, 1sc in each of next 24[26]sts, turn (see 1).

Row 2: sc2tog, 1sc in each of next 21[23]sts, sc2tog, turn.

Row 3: ch1,*1sc in next st, 1dc in next st; repeat from * to last st, 1sc in last st, turn (23[25]sts).

Row 4: ch1, 1sc in next st, *1sc in next st, 1dc in next st; repeat from * to last 2sts, 1sc in each of next 2sts, turn (23[25]sts).

Rows 5–6: repeat Rows 3 and 4.

Row 7 (ankle strap): ch14, 1sc in 7th ch from hook, 1sc in each foll ch, 1sc in each of next 5[6] sts across the Back, sc2tog three times, 1sc in next st, sc2tog three times, 1sc in each of next 5[6]sts. Fasten off (see 2).

Strap right sandal

Skip 2[3]sl sts, from the Back, on the same side as the ankle strap, join yarn in next sl st.

Row 1: ch1, 1sc in same st, 1sc in each of next 2sts, turn, (see 3) *ch13, 1sc in 2nd ch from hook, 1sc in each foll ch, sl st 1 sc; (see 4) repeat from * twice more. Fasten off (see 5). Thread the tapestry needle with same color yarn and seam the straps to the opposite side of the Sole, working on wrong side, and joining them to the sl sts worked to join the Soles,

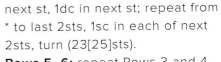

skipping 1[2]sl st from the Back, and leaving 1sl st between each strap (see 6 and 7).

Back left sandal

Work as for right sandal Rows 1–6.

Row 7 (ankle strap): ch1, 1sc in each of next 5[6]sts, sc2tog three times, 1sc in next st, sc2tog three times, 1sc in each of next 5[6]sts, ch14, 1sc in 7th ch from hook, 1sc in each foll ch, sl st in first st of previous row. Fasten off.

Strap left sandal

Skip 4[5]sl sts, from the Back, on the same side as the ankle strap, join yarn in next sl st.

Row 1: ch1, 1sc in same st, 1sc in each of next 2sts, turn, *ch13, 1sc in 2nd ch from hook, 1sc in each foll ch, sl st in next sc; repeat from * twice more. Fasten off. Seam the straps to the opposite side of the Sole in the same way as for the right sandal. Weave in all ends. For each sandal, sew a button on the opposite side to the ankle strap.

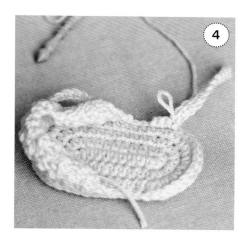

Skill Level: I

Sizes
To fit ages:
0–6 months, sole length 3½in (9cm)
6–12 months, sole length 4in (10cm)
Changes for 6–12 months are in [ ]

Yarn

Main color (MC):
1oz (25g) DK-weight yarn
Shade: Silver
Contrasting color (CC):
1oz (25g) DK-weight yarn
Shade: White

Hooks & Notions
One size D (3.25mm) crochet hook
or size needed to obtain gauge
Four buttons
Tapestry needle

Gauge
10sts and 10 rows in sc to measure
2x2in (5x5cm)

Abbreviations
see page 134

Stitches & Skills
(see Crochet Basics, pages
133–141)
Special stitches used:
sc2tog
Techniques used:
Working rows
Working in rounds
Working in remaining loop
Double Sole 1

grecian sandals

This fine pair of open-toed sandals for boys and girls can be made in any color combination. Taking an ancient classic as inspiration, the design employs a central T-bar to hold the four horizontal straps in place.

The sandals
Follow separate instructions for right and left sandals.
Sole
Make a Double Sole 1 with CC.
Fasten off.

Back

With MC. Join yarn in central st of 9[11]hdc on the side of the Sole. Working in both loops of sl sts used to join the Soles.

Row 1: ch1, 1sc in st at base of ch-1, 1sc in each of next 24[26]sts, turn.

Row 2: sc2tog, 1sc in each of next 21[23]sts, sc2tog, turn.

Row 3: sc2tog, 1sc in each of next 19[21]sts, sc2tog, turn.

Row 4: sc2tog, 1sc in each of next 17[19]sts, sc2tog, turn.

Row 5 for right sandal: ch14, 1sc in 6th ch from hook, 1sc in each of foll 8ch, 1sc in each of next 19[21] sts, turn.

Row 5 for left sandal: Fasten off. Join the yarn on opposite side of the Back in the first stitch, ch14, 1sc in 6th ch from hook, 1sc in each of next 8ch, 1sc in base of ch14, 1sc in each of next 18[20]sts, turn.

Both sandals:

Row 6: ch1, 1sc in each of next 19[21]sts, turn.

Row 7: ch13, 1sc in 6th ch from hook, 1sc in each of foll 7ch, 1sc in each of next 5[6]sts, sc2tog twice, 1sc in next st, sc2tog twice, 1sc in each of next 5[6]sts. Fasten off (see 1).

Front

With MC. Both sandals, both sizes. Skip 1 st from Back, join yarn in next sl st you worked to join Soles.

Strap 1: ch12, skip 6sl sts from Back on opposite side of the Sole, join with sl st in next st (see 2), turn, skip sl st, work 1sc in each

tip

It is important to leave long tails when starting the T-bar and then fastening it off, because these can later be used for seaming the sandal, so allowing for a neater finish with fewer ends to weave in.

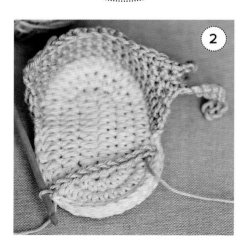

ch, sl st in base of ch-12.
Fasten off (see 3).
Skip next 4sl sts from first strap and start in next st.
Strap 2: ch12, skip 1sl st from Back on opposite side of the Sole, join with sl st in next st (see 4), turn, skip sl st, 1sc in each ch, sl st in base of ch-12, fasten off (see 5).

T-bar

Foundation chain: leaving a long tail, ch20.
Rnd 1: 1sc in 2nd ch from hook, 1sc in each foll ch, rotate work, working along opposite edge in remaining loop, sl st in each st, leaving a long tail, fasten off . Thread needle with first tail, wrap one end of T-bar around front straps and seam strap, working through front straps, so that they stay fixed. Thread another tail and shape loop for ankle straps, working only through T-bar and leaving straps untouched (see 6). Weave in all ends and sew on the buttons.

Sizes
To fit ages:
0–6 months, sole length 3½in (8.5cm)
6–12 months, sole length 3¾in (9.5cm)
Changes for 6–12 months are in [ ]

Yarn

1 oz (25g) 4-ply yarn
Shade: Purple

Hooks & Notions
One size D (3.25mm) crochet hook or size needed to obtain gauge
Tapestry needle
Two buttons

Gauge
11sts and 11 rows in sc to measure 2x2in (5x5cm)

Abbreviations
see page 134

Stitches & Skills
(see Crochet Basics, pages 133–141)
Special stitches used:
sc2tog
v-stitch
Techniques used:
Working in rows
Working in rounds
Joining in yarn
Double Sole 1

bow-front sandals

These striking bow-front sandals make a real statement piece on any day of the week. They work particularly well in strong, bold colors and deserve to be worn with only the best of outfits.

The sandals
Follow separate instructions for right and left sandals.
Sole
Make a Double Sole 1.
Fasten off.

Back

Join yarn in 7th[8th]st of 9[11]hdc on the side of the Sole (see page 100). Working in both loops of sl sts used to join the Soles. Working in both loops of sl sts worked to join Soles.

Row 1: ch1, 1sc in base of ch-1, 1sc in each of next 20[22]sts, turn.

Row 2: ch1, 1sc in each of next 21[23]sts, turn. Repeat Row 2 four times more.

Row 7 for right sandal: ch13, 1sc in 2nd ch from hook, 1sc in each foll

ch, 1sc in each of next sc, 33[35] sc) turn.

Row 7 for left sandal: fasten off, join yarn in on opposite side of Back, ch13, 1sc in 2nd ch from hook, 1sc in each foll ch, 1sc in base of ch-13, 1sc in each next sc to end, (33[35]sc), turn.

Both sandals:

Row 8: ch1, 1sc in each of next 30[32]sc, ch2, skip next 2sc, 1sc in last sc, turn.

Row 9: ch1, 1sc in next sc, 2sc in ch-2 space, 1sc in each of next 10sc, sc2tog 10[11] times. Fasten off (see 1 and 2).

Front

Skip 1[2]sl sts from the Back, join yarn in next sl st (see 3). Both sizes:

Row 1: ch1, 1sc in base of ch-1, 2sc in each of next 7sts, turn.

Row 2: ch3, *skip 2sc, v-stitch in next st; repeat from * three times more, skip next 2sts, 1dc in last st, turn.

Row 3: ch3, *skip next 2 dc, v-stitch in next ch-1 space; repeat from * three times more, skip next

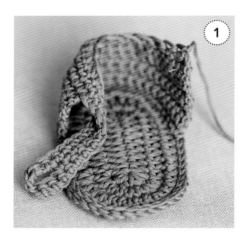

dc, 1dc in 3rd ch of ch-3. Repeat Row 3 four times more.

Row 8: ch1, skip first dc, 1sc in each of next 8dc (skip all ch1) (see 4). With right sides together, the wrong side facing, join Front to opposite side of Sole, starting with the 2nd[3rd]sl st from Back, 1sc in each of next 8sts. Work (see 5). Turn sandal to right side.

T-Strap

Join yarn in 7th stitch of strap (in last loop of foundation chain):

Row 1: ch1, 1sc in base of ch-1, 1sc in each of next 2sts, turn (see 6).

Rows 2–12: ch1, 1sc in each of next 3sts, turn. Fasten off, but leave quite a long tail.

Thread needle with tail, thread T-strap under front section of shoe and turn it back on itself over the top of front section. Seam it, working on wrong side (see 7). Weave in all ends. For each sandal, sew on a button to secure back strap.

Sizes

To fit ages:
0–6 months, sole length 3½in (9cm)
6–12 months, sole length 4in (10cm)
Changes for 6–12 months are in [ ]

Yarn

2oz (50g) Aran-weight yarn
Shade: Chalk white

Hooks & Notions

One size E (3.5mm) crochet hook
or size needed to obtain gauge
Four small buttons

Gauge

9sts and 9 rows in sc to measure
2x2in (5x5cm)

Abbreviations

see page 134

Stitches & Skills

(see Crochet Basics, pages
133–141)
Techniques used:
Working in rounds
Double Sole 2

woven leather sandals

The simplest pair of sandals with a pretty woven upper. Perfect for the newborn baby, these sandals have little straps that crisscross the front of each shoe and are held in place with tiny buttons.

The sandals

Both sandals are made in exactly the same way.

Sole

Make a Double Sole 2.
Don't fasten off, but continue with the Upper.

Upper

Start from last sl st worked to join the Soles, but work in opposite direction.

Rnd 1: ch1 in first sl st, 1sc in each of next 41[45]sts, join with sl st in first sc.

Rnd 2: ch1, 1sc in each of next 7[9]sts, *skip next 2sts, 3dc in next st; repeat from * twice more, skip next 2sts, 1sc in each of next 23[25]sts, join with sl st in first sc (see 1).

Rnd 3: ch1, 1sc in each of next 5[7] sts, skip next 2sc, skip next dc, 3dc in next dc, *skip next 2dc, 3dc in next dc; repeat from * once more, skip next dc, skip next 2sc, 1sc in each of next 21[23]sts, join with sl st in first sc.

Rnd 4: ch1, 1sc in each of next 3[5] sts, skip next 2sc, skip next dc, 3dc in next dc, *skip next 2dc, 3dc in next dc; repeat from * once more, skip next dc, skip next 2sc, 1sc in each of next 3[5]sts, 1dc in each of next 16sts, join with sl st in first sc (see 2). Don't fasten off, but continue working straps as folls:

Straps

ch13[14], 1sc in 7th ch from hook, 1sc in each foll ch, continue to work 1sc in each of next 16dc across the Back, ch13[14], 1sc in 7th ch from hook, 1sc in each foll ch, sl st in last dc of previous rnd. Fasten off (see 3).

Weave in all ends. For each sandal, sew buttons on the first and last group of 3dc.

Sizes
To fit ages:
0–6 months, sole length 3½in (9cm)
6–12 months, sole length 4in (10cm)
Changes for 6–12 months are in [ ]

Yarn

Main color (MC):
2oz (50g) DK-weight yarn
Shade: Pink
Contrasting color (CC):
Small amount DK-weight yarn
Shade: Dark gray

Hooks & Notions
One size D (3.25mm) crochet hook
or size needed to obtain gauge
Tapestry needle
Pins (optional)
Two small buttons

Gauge
10sts and 10 rows in sc to measure
2x2in (5x5cm)

Abbreviations
see page 134

Stitches & Skills
(see Crochet Basics, pages
133–141)
Special stitches used:
sc2tog
Techniques used:
Working in rows
Working in rounds
Double Sole 1

ruffle-front sandals

Footwear with flair, these ruffle-front sandals put the finishing touch to the prettiest outfits. They are bound to be the focus of attention at any special occasion—even a teddybears' picnic on the bedroom floor.

The sandals
Follow separate instructions for making right and left sandals.
Sole
Make a Double Sole 1.
Fasten off.

Back

With MC.

Join yarn in 7th[8th]st of 9[11]hdc on the side of the Sole (see 1). Working in both loops of the sl sts worked to join the Soles.

Row 1: ch1, 1sc in base of ch-1, 1sc in each of next 20[22]sts, turn.

Row 2: ch1, 1sc in each of next 21[23]sts, turn.

Rows 3–6: repeat Row 2 four times more.

Row 7 for right sandal: ch14, 1sc in 7th ch from hook, 1sc in each foll ch, 1sc in each of next 6[7]sts, sc2tog four times, 1sc in each of next 7[8]sts. Fasten off (see 2).

Row 7 for left sandal: ch1, 1sc in each of next 7[8]sts, sc2tog four times, 1sc in each of next 6[7]sts, ch14, 1sc in 7th ch from hook, 1sc in each foll ch, sl st in first st of previous row. Fasten off (see 3).

Front

Sl sts at the end of each row that you worked in sl st when joining the Soles. Skip 8[9]sl sts from the Back, join yarn in next st, ch8, skip next 7sts, sl st in each of next 2sts along the Sole, turn (see 4).

The rest of the pattern is the same for both sizes.

Row 1: skip 2sl sts along the Sole, 1sc in each of next 8ch, sl st in each of next 2sl sts along the Sole, turn. Continue skipping sl sts and working sl sts in the patt set.

Row 2: skip 2sl sts, working into back loops only, 1sc in next 8sts, sl st in each of next 2sl sts, turn.

9 8 7 6 5 4 3 2 1

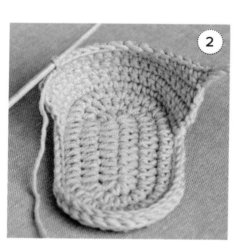

Row 3: skip 2sl sts, working into both loops, 2sc in next st, 1sc in each of next 6sts, 2sc in last sc, sl st in each of next 2sts, turn.

Row 4: skip 2sl sts, working into back loops only, 1sc in each of next 10sts, sl st in each of next 2sts, turn.

Row 5: skip 2sl sts, working into both loops, 1sc in each of next 10sts, sl st in each of next 2sts. Repeat Rows 4 and 5 once more, but in the last row work only one sl st. Fasten off (see 5).

T-bar

Working in the 4 centermost stitches of the Front.

Row 1: ch1, 1sc in base of ch-1, 1sc in each of next 3sts, turn.

Row 2: ch1, 1sc in each of next 4sts, turn.

Rows 3–12: repeat Row 2 ten times more. Fasten off, but leave a long tail.

Thread the needle with the tail, shape the loop for the ankle strap, and seam it. The loop must be small—just big enough to pass through the ankle strap (see 6).

Ruffle

Foundation chain: ch13.

Row 1: 1sc in 2nd ch from hook, 1sc in each of next 11ch, turn.

Rnd 1: ch3, 3dc in each of next 11sts, ch3, sl st in base of last st, rotate work and work along opposite edge in base of the Foundation chain, sl st in first st, ch3, 3dc in each of next 11sts, ch3, sl st in base of last st.

Fasten off (see 7).
Place the ruffle on the front of the sandal (you can pin it, if that helps) and, starting below the loop for the ankle strap, join the ruffle to the Front, working evenly sl sts across the center of the ruffle.
Fasten off (see 8). Change to CC and work sc evenly around the ruffle (see 9).
Weave in all ends. For each sandal, sew a button on each side, for securing the strap.

tip

If you find it too complicated to join the ruffle to the front of the sandal using sl st, you can always sew the ruffle on using a tapestry needle and making a seam instead.

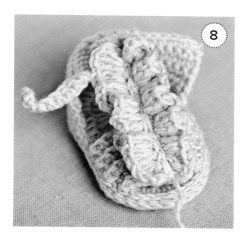

comfort sandals

Every tot could do with a pair of these. With their closed backs, ankle straps, and sturdy front straps, these two-tone sandals offer the best support for everyday wear.

Skill Level: II

Sizes
To fit ages:
0–6 months, sole length 3½in (9cm)
6–12 months, sole length 4in (10cm)
Changes for 6–12 months are in [ ]

Yarn

Main color (MC):
1oz (25g) DK-weight yarn
Shade: Green
Contrasting color (CC):
1oz (25g) DK-weight yarn
Shade: Light brown

Hooks & Notions
One size D (3.25mm) crochet hook
or size needed to obtain gauge
Two buttons
Tapestry needle

Gauge
10sts and 10 rows in sc to measure
2x2in (5x5cm)

Abbreviations
see page 134

Stitches & Skills
(see Crochet Basics, pages
133–141)
Special stitches used:
sc2tog
Techniques used:
Working in rows
Working in rounds
Joining in yarn
Double Sole 1

The sandals
Follow separate instructions for right
and left sandals.
Sole
Make a Double Sole 1
with CC.

Back

With MC. Join yarn in center stitch of 9[11]hdc on the side of the Sole. Working in both loops of the sl sts worked to join the Soles.

Row 1: ch1, 1sc in base of ch-1, 1sc in each of next 24[26]sts, turn.

Row 2: sc2tog, 1sc in each of next 21[23]sts, sc2tog, turn.

Row 3: sc2tog, 1sc in each of next 19[21]sts, sc2tog, turn.

Row 4: sc2tog, 1sc in each of next 17[19]sts, sc2tog, turn.

Row 5: ch2, skip first st, 1dc in

each of next 18[20]sts, turn.

Row 6: sc2tog, 1sc in each of next 16[18]sts, turn. Don't fasten off, but continue to work ankle strap:

For right sandal: ch17[19], 1sc in 9th ch from hook, 1sc in each foll ch 1sc in each of next 17[19]sts. Fasten off (see 1).

For left sandal: ch1, 1sc in each of next 17[19]sts, ch17[19], 1sc in 9th ch from hook, 1sc in each foll ch, sl st in first sc of previous row. Fasten off.

Front strap

With MC. Both sandals. Skip next 2[3]sts from the Heel, join the yarn in next st. Working in both loops of sl sts you worked to join the Soles.

Row 1: ch1, 1sc in base of ch-1, 1sc in each of next 2sts, turn (see 2).

Row 2: ch1, 1sc in each of next 3sts, turn.

Rows 3– 12: repeat Row 2 ten times more.

Working on wrong side, on opposite side of the Sole, skip

2[3]sl sts from Heel, join strap to next 3sts working 1sc in each st through all four loops (see 3). Don't fasten off, but turn sandal to right side and work evenly sc across row ends of the front strap. Fasten off. Repeat along opposite side of the strap. Join in CC to the base of the first sc st worked across the row ends of front strap. Work sl sts across strap, working into the base of sc sts (see 4). Fasten off. Repeat along opposite side of the front strap (see 5).

T-bar

With MC. Join yarn in 4th[5th]st of ankle strap, and work:

Row 1: ch1, 1sc in base of ch-1, 1sc in each of next 2sc, turn.

Row 2: ch1, 1sc in each of next 3sc, turn.

Repeat Rows 2 five[six] times (see 6). Fasten off, leaving a long tail. Thread needle with tail and sew T-strap to center of front strap, working on wrong side (see 7). Weave in ends. Sew a button onto each shoe, to fasten ankle strap.

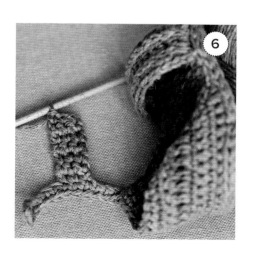

espadrilles

Skill Level: II

Sizes
To fit ages:
0–6 months, sole length 3½in (8.5cm)
6–12 months, sole length 3¾in (9.5cm)
Changes for 6–12 months are in [ ]

Yarn

3

Main color (MC):
1oz (25g) DK-weight yarn
Shade: Light brown
Contrasting color (CC):
1oz (25g) DK-weight yarn
Shade: Red

Hooks & Notions
One size D (3.25mm) crochet hook or size needed to obtain gauge
Tapestry needle
Four buttons

Gauge
11sts and 11 rows in sc to measure 2x2in (5x5cm)

Abbreviations
see page 134

Stitches & Skills
(see Crochet Basics, pages 133–141)
Special stitches used:
sc2tog
Techniques used:
Working in rows
Working in rounds
Working in front and back loops
Working in the remaining loop
Joining in yarn
Double Sole 1

A summer vacation would be dull without these adorable espadrilles. With their "woven-rope" soles and "canvas" uppers, these chic sandals are the only footwear to be seen in on the golden sands at the beach.

The sandals
Both sandals are made in exactly the same way.
Sole
Make a Double Sole 1.
Fasten off.

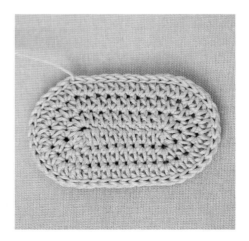

Back

With MC.

Join yarn in central st of 9[11]hdc on the side of the Sole. Working in both loops of sl sts used to join the Soles.

Row 1: ch1, 1sc in st at base of ch-1, 1sc in each of next 24[26]sts, turn.

Row 2: sc2tog, 1sc in each of next 21[23]sts, sc2tog, turn.

Row 3: sc2tog, 1sc in each of next 19[21]sts, sc2tog, turn.

Row 4: sc2tog, 1sc in each of next 17[19]sts, sc2tog, turn.

Row 5: sc2tog, 1sc in each of next 15[17]sts, sc2tog, turn.

Row 6: sc2tog, 1sc in each of next 13[15]sts, sc2tog, turn.

Row 7: sc2tog, 1sc in each of next 11[13]sts, sc2tog, turn.

Row 8: sc2tog, 1sc in each of next 9[11]sts, sc2tog. (11[13]sts)
Fasten off.

Edging

With MC. Join yarn in edge st at base of Back, work sc evenly across the rows ends.
Repeat along the other edge.
Fasten off. (see 1).

Front

With CC. For both sizes.

Mark 7 centermost stitches of Toe. With right side facing, join yarn into the st furthest to the right of the marked sts. Working in sl sts worked to join the Soles, continue as folls:

Row 1: ch1, 1sc in base of ch-1, *ch1, 1sc in next st; repeat from * five times more, sl st in each of next 2sts along the Sole, turn (see 2).

Row 2: skip 2sl sts, 1sc in next sc, 1sc in next ch-1 space, *ch1, skip next sc, 1sc in next ch-1 space; repeat from * four times more, 1sc in last sc, sl st in each of next 2 sts along the Sole, turn.

Row 3: skip 2sl sts, 1sc in next sc, *ch1, skip next sc, 1sc in next ch-1 space; repeat from * five times more, sl st in each of next 2sl sts along the Sole, turn.

Row 4: repeat Row 2.
Row 5: skip 2sl sts, 1sc in next sc, *ch1, skip next sc, 1sc in next ch-1 space; repeat from * five times more, sl st in next sl st along the Sole, turn.
Row 6: skip sl st, 1sc in next sc, 1sc in next ch-1 space, *ch1, skip next sc, 1sc in next ch-1 space; repeat from * four times more, 1sc in last sc, sl st in next sl st along the Sole, turn.
Row 7: skip sl st, 1sc in next sc, *ch1, skip next sc, 1sc in next ch-1

space; repeat from * five times more, sl st in next sl st along the Sole, turn.
Rows 8–9: repeat Rows 6 and 7 once more.
Row 10: repeat Row 6 once more.
Row 11: skip sl st, work sl st in each st. Fasten off (see 3).

Strap
For both sizes.
Foundation chain: ch13.
Rnd 1: 1sc in 2nd ch from hook, 1sc in each foll ch, rotate work, working along the opposite edge into remaining loop, 1sc in each st, (see 4).
Rnd 2: ch5, sl st in each of next 12sts, ch5, skip next st, rotate the work, working along the opposite edge, sl st in each of next 11sts. Fasten off (see 5).
Weave in all ends. For each sandal, sew a button on each side at the back, for securing the strap.

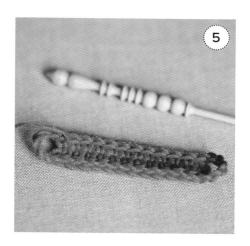

Skill Level: II

Sizes
To fit ages:
0–6 months, sole length 3½in (9cm)
6–12 months, sole length 4in (10cm)
Changes for 6–12 months are in [ ]

Yarn

Main color (MC):
2oz (50g) DK-weight yarn
Shade: Light brown
Contrasting color (CC):
Small amounts DK-weight yarn
Shades: Bright green, pink

Hooks & Notions
One size D (3.25mm) crochet hook
or size needed to obtain gauge
Tapestry needle

Gauge
10sts and 10 rows in sc to measure
2x2in (5x5cm)

Abbreviations
see page 134

Stitches & Skills
(see Crochet Basics, pages
133–141)
Techniques used:
Working in rows
Working in rounds
Working in front and back loops
Working in remaining loop
Joining in yarn
Double Sole 1

flowery sandals

Summer parties and picnics in the garden—that's what these sandals are all about. It's a clever design, in which the whole front section is a pink flower encircled by leaves. Make the flower in any color you like.

The sandals
Both sandals are made in exactly the same way.
Sole
Make a Double Sole 1 with MC.
Fasten off.

Flower

With CC (pink). **Foundation ring:** ch4, join with sl st in first ch.

Rnd 1: ch1, 8sc into ring, join with sl st in first sc.

Rnd 2: working in front loops only, *ch3, sl st in next st; repeat from * seven times more (eight petals).

Rnd 3: *4sc in next petal; repeat from * to end, join with sl st in first sc of Rnd. Fasten off (see 1).

Leaves

With CC (green). Join yarn in the back loop of Rnd 2 of Flower.

Rnd 1: *ch8, sl st in next st* (see 2), repeat from * seven times more. (eight leaves)

Rnd 2: 6sc in first leaf, join with sl st in 7th[9th]sl st of Sole (see 3), 6sc in same leaf, *6sc in next petal, skip next 2sl sts of Sole, join with sl st in next st, 6sc in same leaf; repeat from * six times more, (see 4), join with sl st in first sc of next petal. Fasten off.

Back strap

With CC (green). Join yarn in 2nd st of last leaf.

Row 1: ch1, 1sc in same st, 1sc in each of next 2sts, turn (see 5).
Row 2: ch1, 1sc in each of next 3sts, turn. Repeat Row 2 20[24] times more. Wrong side facing, join strap to first leaf with sl sts, starting with 2nd sc (see 6).

Heel strap

With CC (green). Mark 4 centermost stitches of back of sandal. With right side facing, join yarn into the st furthest to the right of the marked sts.

Row 1: ch1, 1sc in base of ch-1, 1sc in each of next 3sts, turn (see 7).
Row 2: ch1, 1sc in each of next 4sts, turn.
Rows 3–13: repeat Row 2, eleven times more.
Wrap heel strap around back strap, join last row to first row, working sl st in each st and fasten off (see 8). Alternatively, leaving tail, fasten off after Row 13, stitch a seam using the tapestry needle. Weave in all ends.

Sizes
To fit ages:
0–6 months, sole length 3½in (9cm)
6–12 months, sole length 4in (10cm)
Changes for 6–12 months are in [ ]

Yarn

2oz (50g) DK-weight yarn
Shade: Pink

Hooks & Notions
One size D (3.25mm) crochet hook
or size needed to obtain gauge
Tapestry needle

Gauge
10sts and 10 rows in sc to measure
2x2in (5x5cm)

Abbreviations
see page 134

Stitches & Skills
(see Crochet Basics, pages
133–141)
Special stitches used:
sc2tog
Techniques used:
Working in rows
Working in rounds
Joining in yarn
Double Sole 1

pompom slippers

This wonderful pair of cozy pompom slippers makes the perfect choice for lounging around at home in style. This fluffy design works best in soft cotton-candy shades.

The slippers
Both slippers are made in exactly the same way.
Sole
Make a Double Sole 1.
Fasten off.

Heel

Join yarn in central st of 9[11]hdc on the side of the Sole. Working in both loops of sl sts used to join the Soles.

Row 1: ch1, 1sc in st at base of ch-1, 1sc in each of next 24[26]sts, turn.

Row 2: sc2tog, 1sc in each of next 21[23]sts, sc2tog, turn.

Row 3: sc2tog, 1sc in each of next 19[21]sts, sc2tog, turn.

Row 4: sc2tog, 1sc in each of next 17[19]sts, sc2tog, turn.

Row 5: sc2tog, 1dc in each of next 15[17]sts, sc2tog. Don't fasten off. Continue as folls for both sizes.

Straps

First strap: Row 1: ch1, work 4sc evenly across the rows ends of Heel (see 1), turn.

Row 2–12: ch1, 1sc in each of next 4 sts, turn. Fasten off. Second strap: Repeat first strap across row ends of opposite side of Heel (see 2).

Edging

Join yarn with right side facing, in edge st, at base of the right-hand side of Heel. Work sc evenly around first strap, across the Back, and around second strap. Fasten off. Turn the sandal inside out and working in sl sts made to join the Soles, join strap to Sole, leave 2sl sts unworked from Back and work in next 4sts, sl st in each st through both layers. Fasten off. Work second strap in the same way. Straps overlap differently on each sandal (see 3, 4).

Flower

Foundation ring: ch4, join with sl st.

Rnd 1: ch1, 9sc into ring, 1sl st in first sc.

Rnd 2: working in back loops only, ch1, 2sc in each st (18sc), join with sl st in first sc.

Rnd 3: working in back loops only, *(1sl st, ch6, 1sl st) in next sc; repeat from * to end (18 petals made) (see 5).

Rnd 4: working in front loops only of Rnd 2 (1sl st, ch6, 1sc) in front loop of first sc, *(1sc, ch6, 1sc) in front loop of next sc (18 petals made); repeat from * to end, sl st in 1st sl st of round.

Rnd 5: working in front loops only of Rnd 1 (see 6), (1sl st, ch6, 1sc) in front loop of first sc, *(1sc, ch6, 1sc) in remaining loop of next sc; repeat from * to end, sl st in 1st sl st of round (9 petals made) (see 7). Fasten off, leaving a long tail. Thread needle with tail and, working through both layers of front, sew flower onto the sandal. Weave in all ends.

Skill Level: III

Sizes

To fit ages:
0–6 months, sole length 3½in (9cm)
6–12 months, sole length 4in (10cm)
Changes for 6–12 months are in [ ]

Yarn

Main color (MC):
1oz (25g) DK-weight yarn
Shade: Light brown

Contrasting color (CC):
1oz (25g) Aran-weight yarn
Shade: Chalk white

Hooks & Notions

One size D (3.25mm) crochet hook
or size needed to obtain gauge
Two buttons
Tapestry needle

Gauge

10sts and 10 rows in sc to measure
2x2in (5x5cm)

Abbreviations

see page 134

Stitches & Skills

Special stitches used:
(see Crochet Basics, pages
133–141)
Techniques used:
Working in rows
Working in rounds
Joining in yarn
Double Sole 1

gladiator sandals

This handsome pair of gladiator sandals is ideal footwear for the intrepid adventurer. What else to put on when on the lookout for a lion to do battle with?

The sandals

Follow separate instructions for right and left sandals.
Sole
Make a Double Sole 1 with CC.
Fasten off.

Front

With MC. Mark 7 centermost stitches of Toe. With right side facing, join yarn into the st furthest to the right of the marked sts.

Row 1: ch1, 1sc in st at base of ch-1, 1sc in each of next 6sts, turn.

Row 2: ch1, skip next st, 1sc in each of next 6sts, turn.

Row 3: ch1, skip next st, 1sc in each of next 5sts, turn.

Row 4: ch1, skip next st, 1sc in each of next 4sts, turn.

Row 5: ch1, skip next st, 1sc in each of next 3sts, turn.

Row 6: ch1, 1sc in each of next 3sts, turn. Repeat Row 6 thirteen[fifteen] times more. Fasten off (see 1).

First strap

With MC. Join yarn in the 4th[5th] st from the Front.

Row 1: ch1, 1sc in st at base of ch-1, 1sc in each of next 2sts, turn (see 2).

Rows 2–12: ch1, 1sc in each of next 3sts, turn. On the opposite side, skip 3sl sts from Front, join strap to next 3sts, working on wrong side, sl st in each of the next 3sl sts used to join Soles. Fasten off (see 3).

Heel and remaining straps

With MC. Join yarn in the 4th st from the first strap.

Rnd 1: ch1, 1sc in st at base of ch-1, 1sc in each of next 20[22]sts, ch12, join with sl st in first sc (see 4).

Rnd 2: ch1, 1sc in st at base of

ch-1, 1sc in each of next 32[34]sts, join with sl st in first sc.

Rnd 3: ch1, 1sc in each of next 33[35]sts, join with sl st in first sc. Continue to work in rows:

Row 1: ch1, 1sc in each of next 21[23]sts, turn.

Rows 2 −3: Repeat Row 1.

Row 4 for right sandal: ch12, 1sc in 2nd ch from hook, 1sc in each foll ch, 1sc in each of next 21[23] sts across the Back, turn.

Row 5 for right sandal: ch1, 1sc in each of next 32[34]sts.

Fasten off (see 5).

Row 4 for left sandal: fasten off and join the yarn in first sc on opposite side of the Heel, ch12, 1sc in 2nd ch from hook, 1sc in each foll ch, 1sc in in base of ch-12, 1sc in each of next 20[22]sts across the Back, turn.

Row 5 for left sandal: ch1, 1sc in each of next 32[34]sts. Fasten off.

Edging

With CC. Join yarn in edge st at base of Front, work sc evenly across the rows ends, along the last row, across the row ends. Fasten off (see 6). Join yarn in edge st at base of the first strap, work sc evenly across the rows ends. Fasten off. Repeat along the opposite edge. (see 7). Repeat along the lower edge of the second strap. Join yarn in edge st at base of the upper edge of the second strap, work sc evenly across row ends of the second strap, Heel, along the Back to

the end of the ankle strap, ch7
(to shape the button loop), rotate
work, sc evenly along opposite
edge to the beg of round.
Fasten off (see 8).

Using MC thread and a tapestry
needle, sew Front to first two
straps (with back stitch seam)
(see 9), following line of stitches
made with MC. From end of Front,
shape a loop for ankle strap. Stitch
it (see 10). Weave in all ends and
sew on the buttons.

tip

Once you start
working on the straps,
you can hide some of
the tails from the straps
between the Soles. To
do this, insert the crochet
hook through the top
Sole only, and pull
the tail inside.

crochet basics

Before you start crocheting your super cute shoes, boots, and sandals, gather together everything you will need for your project. You might also find it helpful to read over the crochet basics discussed in this chapter before beginning, and always remember to test your gauge before you start. Happy crocheting!

Basic crochet kit

Crochet hooks come in a great variety of materials—from wood and plastic to steel and ivory—and in different shapes and sizes. The projects in this book use one of two hook sizes: U.S. size D (3.25mm) and U.S. size E (3.5mm). Always use the size of hook listed in the pattern. For footwear, using a small size allows you to crochet tightly and produce a sturdier shoe with a better shape.

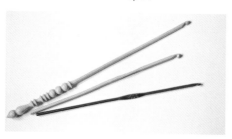

Ruler or size gauge for checking the hook size and gauge at the beginning of the project and the lengths of the finished pieces.

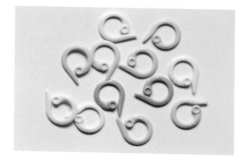

Stitch markers are useful for marking certain stitches in rows, or to mark the first stitch when working in rounds.

Small sharp scissors for cutting the yarn and trimming ends when finishing.

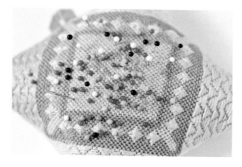

Glass-headed pins can be useful when seaming different sections together.

Tapestry needle for seaming and finishing. Choose one with a large eye for easy threading.

Yarn

Well-spun yarns produce neat, tidy results. Most of the projects in this book use either DK- or worsted-weight yarn. For some details you will also need sportweight yarn. Shades of yarn have been given for each pattern, but you can replace them with a shade of your choice, as long as you match the gauge indicated in the pattern. For the best results use natural yarns, such as wool or cotton, or blended yarns. Avoid 100% acrylic yarn for shoe-like booties, especially for the ones without any straps or other means of fastening, as acrylic yarn doesn't keep its shape as well as natural yarns do. For a list of the specific yarns used in these projects, turn to page 142.

Yarn key

 Superfine/4-ply
 Fine/Sportweight/Baby
 Light/DK/8-ply
 Medium/Aran/Worsted/
12-ply
 Bulky/Chunky
Super bulky/Craft weight

Reading patterns

If you are new to crochet patterns, you may feel that they are written in a different language. However, you will soon begin to recognize the abbreviations used. Essentially, they make the patterns shorter and easier to follow.

Crochet abbreviations

beg	begin/beginning
bet	between
BP dc	back post double crochet
CC	contrasting color
ch	chain stitch
CL	cluster
cm	centimeter(s)
dc	double crochet
dc2tog	double crochet two stitches together
dtr	double treble crochet
dec	decrease/decreasing/ decreases
foll	follow/follows/following
FP dc	front post double crochet
hdc	half double crochet
inc	increase/increases/ increasing
MC	main color
mm	millimeter
rep	repeat(s)
sc	single crochet
sc2tog	single crochet two stitches together
sk	skip/miss
sl st	slip stitch
st(s)	stitch(es)
tog	together
tr	treble
yo	yarn over hook
*	repeat the step

Crochet techniques

Crochet is all about combining really simple techniques with a number of more elaborate flourishes. Once you have mastered making chains, you are ready to progress to a variety of fancy stitches.

Holding the hook and yarn

Learning to hold the hook and yarn correctly is the first step to successful crochet. Most people hold the hook as they would a pencil or a knife, but you should experiment to find the most comfortable way for you.

Mastering the slipknot

Making a slipknot is the first step in any project. Master this technique, and you are on your way to super crochet! Make a loop in the yarn. With your hook, catch the ball end of the yarn and draw it through the loop. Pull firmly on the yarn and hook to tighten the knot and create your first loop.

Making a chain (ch)

Before making a chain, you need to place the slipknot on a hook. Now hold the tail end of the yarn with your left hand and bring the yarn over the hook (yo) by passing the hook in front of the yarn, under it, and around it. Keeping the yarn taut, draw the hook and yarn through the loop made by

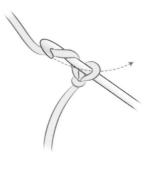

the slipknot, ensuring that the stitch stays fairly loose. Repeat to make the number of chain stitches (ch) required. As the chain lengthens, keep hold of the bottom edge to maintain tension.

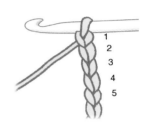

How to count a chain

To count the stitches, use the "right side" of your work. This is the side with the more visible "V" shapes. Do not count the original slipknot, but count each "V" as one chain.

Making a slip stitch (sl st)

A slip stitch (sl st) is used to join one stitch to another—say, when joining a circle. It is usually made by picking up two strands of a stitch. However, when it is worked into the starting chain, you only pick up the back loop. Insert the hook into the back loop of the next stitch and pass yarn over hook (yo), as in the chain stitch (ch). Draw the yarn through both loops on the hook and repeat.

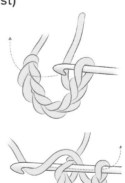

Working in rounds
Making a chain ring
Work a chain as long as required by the pattern. Join the last chain stitch (ch) to the first with a slip stitch (sl st). Begin the first round by working into the chain ring.

Working around basic chain
When making a sole, you need to work around the basic chain. First work in each ch to the last ch. Then work the indicated number of stitches into the last ch, turn, and continue to work in remaining loop of the basic chain to the last ch. Again, work the indicated number of stitches into the last ch and join the round with sl st into the indicated stitch.

Working in front loop, in back loop, or remaining loop
On the top of each stitch there are two loops. The one farthest from you as you look at the stitch is the back loop, and the one closest to you is the front loop. When working in the basic chain, one loop will remain at the bottom of the work—this is a remaining loop.

front loop

back loop

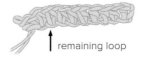
remaining loop

Joining in yarn
When joining in yarn in the middle of the work, complete the last step with the new yarn. For example, when changing color, if you are working single crochet (see below), work Step 1 with MC, but yo and work Step 2 in CC.

Basic stitches
Single crochet (sc)
1. Insert the hook, front to back, into the next stitch, yo. Draw through one loop to front; there should be two loops on the hook, yo.
2. Draw through both loops to complete single crochet (sc).

Double crochet (dc)
This makes a more open fabric, because the stitches are taller.
1. Wrap the yarn over the hook from back to front (yo). Insert the hook into the next stitch, from front to back, yo again and draw through the stitch.
2. There should be three loops on the hook, yo and pull through two loops.
3. There should be two loops on the hook, yo, and pull through the remaining two loops to complete the stitch.

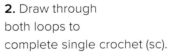

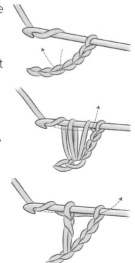

Half-double (hdc)

The half-double is simply that: half of a double crochet. Therefore, the stitch is slightly shorter than double crochet. In step 2 of double crochet, pull through all the remaining loops in one movement.

Special stitches

Single crochet two stitches together (sc2tog)

Begin to work sc, but don't complete it, leaving two loops on hook. Insert hook in next st and pull the yarn through it so that you now have three loops on hook, yo and pull through all three loops on the hook to complete the stitch.

Double crochet two stitches together (dc2tog)

Begin to work dc in next st, but don't complete it, leaving two loops on hook. Work another incomplete dc in next st, so that you now have three loops on the hook, yo and pull through all three loops on the hook to complete the stitch.

Double crochet eight stitches together (dc8tog)

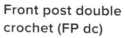

Begin to work dc in next st, but don't complete it, leaving two loops on hook.

Work incomplete dc in next 7sts, so that you now have nine loops on the hook, yo, pull through all nine loops on the hook and work ch to complete the stitch.

To work dc10tog, dc11tog, and dc12tog, follow the same steps as for dc8tog, only instead of 8sts, work 10, 11, or 12sts together.

Crab stitch

When last row is complete, do not turn the work around, *insert the hook in first st to the right, yo and pull it through st, yo and pull it through two loops on the hook; repeat from * to end.

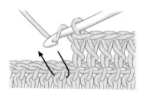

Front post double crochet (FP dc)

Yo, insert hook from front to back around post of next st, yo and pull through so that you have three loops on the hook. Complete the stitch as normal dc.

Back post double crochet (BP dc)

Yo, insert hook from back to front around post of next st, yo and pull through so that you have three loops on the hook. Complete the stitch as normal dc.

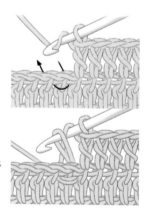

V-stitch
(dc, ch, dc) in specified stitch.

Cluster (CL)
*Yo, insert hook in specified stitch and draw up a loop, yo, and draw through two loops; repeat from * twice more, yo and draw through all four loops.

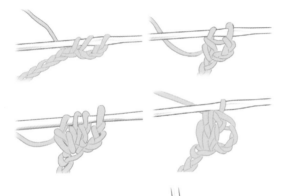

Cluster shell (CL shell)
(CL, ch3, CL, ch3, CL, ch3, CL) in specified stitch.

Shell
(dc, ch2, dc, ch2, dc) in specified stitch.

Finishing
Fastening off
1. After fastening off the last st, snip off the yarn from the ball, leaving approximately 2in (5cm) to weave in.
2. Draw through the last loop and pull tightly to fasten.

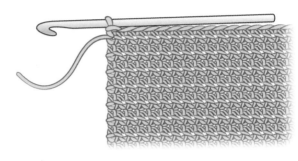

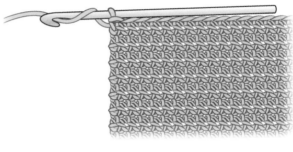

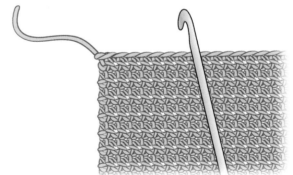

Weaving in ends

1. Use the hook to draw the yarn through at least five stitches, weaving the yarn over and under as you go to secure the yarn. A tapestry needle can also be used, as pictured.
2. Snip off the excess yarn.

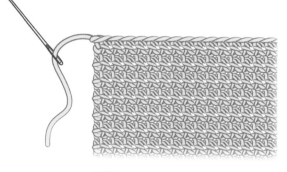

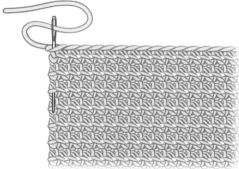

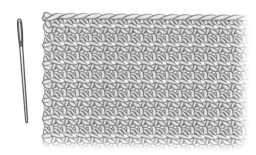

Making a twisted cord

Cut a length of yarn that measures four times the desired length of the finishing twisted cord. Hang the cord, at its center, over a hook or door handle. Begin twisting the two strands of yarn together using your fingers. The tighter the yarns are twisted, the firmer the finished cord will be—this will also reduce the length of the finished cord, however. Remove the cord from the hook and, holding it at the center, bring the two loose ends together. They should twist around each other. Pull the resulting cord taut, to smooth it out, knot both ends, and trim.

Backstitch

A number of projects in this book require the stitching together of some seams. Backstitch is ideal for this. The following method shows how to do backstitch from right to left.
1. Bring the needle up through the work and make a stitch going to the right.
2. Now bring up the needle to the left of the beginning of the first stitch, at stitch-length distance.
3. Make a stitch going to the right, which meets the start of the first stitch.
4. Repeat to the end of the row.

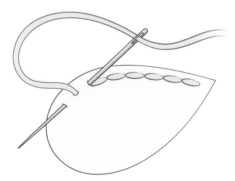

Soles

Almost all of the projects in this book start with making a sole. Sole 1 is used for projects made using DK-weight yarn, while Sole 2 is used for projects made using Aran (worsted-weight) yarn. For either type, at the end of each round, you have to join in the first hdc and start the next round with the next stitch, not with the one you joined in to complete the previous round. Follow the instructions for each project to see whether or not to fasten off having made the sole.

A double sole is used for some of the boots and all of the sandals. The uppers of the sandals are lightweight, since they consist mainly of straps, so a double sole helps to make the shoe sturdier, more resistant, and generally better shaped. The majority of sandals are made using DK-weight yarn, and so require Double Sole 1. The only exception to this is the Woven Leather Sandals (see pages 105–106), which are made using Aran (worsted-weight) yarn, and so require Double Sole 2. When making double soles always take care that you work the right amount of sl sts to join them together. This is essential for keeping the counts right when working on the uppers.

Sole 1

To fit ages:

0–6 months, sole length 3½in (9cm)
6–12 months, sole length 4in (10cm)
Changes for size 6–12 months are in [ ]

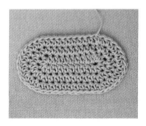

Rnd 1: ch11 [13], hdc in 3rd ch from hook, hdc in next 7[9]sts, 6hdc in last ch, work on opposite side, hdc in next 7[9]sts, 5hdc in last ch, join with sl st in first hdc.

Rnd 2: ch1, hdc in next 8[10]sts, 2hdc in each of next 5sts, hdc in next 8[10]sts, 2hdc in each of next 5sts, join with sl st in first hdc.

Rnd 3: ch1, hdc in next 8[10]sts, *2hdc in next st, 1hdc in next st; repeat from * four times more, hdc in next 8[10]sts, repeat from *5 times more, join with sl st in first hdc.

Sole 2

To fit ages:

0–6 months, sole length 3½in (9cm)
6–12 months, sole length 4in (10cm)
Changes for size 6–12 months are in [ ]

Rnd 1: 9[11]ch, hdc in 3rd ch from hook, hdc in next 5[7]sts, 6hdc in last ch, work on opposite side, hdc in next 5[7]sts, 5hdc in last ch, join with sl st in first hdc.

Rnd 2: 1ch, hdc in next 6[8]sts, 2hdc in each of next 5sts, hdc in next 6[8]sts, 2hdc in each of next 5sts, join with sl st in first hdc.

Rnd 3: 1ch, hdc in next 6[8]sts, (2hdc in next st, 1hdc in next st) five times, hdc in next 6[8]sts, (2hdc in next st, 1hdc in next st) five times, join with sl st in first hdc.

Double soles

To make a double sole, follow the project pattern to see whether you need to make Sole 1 or Sole 2. In each case the making up is the same.

Start by making two soles. Fasten off the first sole, but not the second (see 1). Place

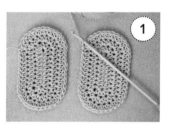

the soles wrong sides together, pull the loop you left open through the second sole (see 2), and join both soles together, working sl sts around (work in all four loops), 46[50] sl sts for Double Sole 1 and 42[46]sl sts for Double Sole 2. Fasten off (see 3).

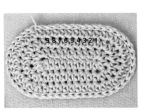

Note: When working with double soles, for most of the projects, you have to begin the upper on the side of the sole. There are 9[11]sts at the center and each pattern will stipulate whether to begin in the central stitch (or another stitch). You should count stitches from right to left as shown.

Making a nonslip sole

You don't need to worry about nonslip soles until a baby takes his or her first steps. However, once the first attempts at walking are made, nonslip soles are highly recommended. There are various ways to make them.

Suede sole Cut a sole from suede and use a large tapestry needle to make holes all around the edge. They need to be large enough that you can insert a crochet hook into them and work a stitch. You need to make a hole for each of the stitches in the first round of shoe's upper. With the sole complete, skip the pattern instructions for the sole, and crochet the upper part using the suede sole as a base. For the first round, use as small a hook as possible—it will be easier to insert into the holes. Switch to the hook indicated in the pattern for subsequent rounds.

Adding tread You can sew something onto the sole, such as big pieces of elastic or trim, to give the sole a rough tread. There are also special stickers available from craft stores that you can use.

Puff paint It is possible to buy a product known as puff paint, which you apply as dots to the sole of the shoe. Some products need heat treatment (using an iron) to make them puff, while others do not. Start by making the crochet sole—it is best to make both soles at the same to save the time while the paint dries. Fasten off the sole, but do not make it too tight. This way, you can open the fastened loop (if required by the pattern) and continue to crochet the upper part once the sole is ready. Be sure that you will not need to make any modifications to the sole. Follow the manufacturer's instructions to apply puff paint. Once the paint has puffed, you can start work on the upper parts.

The projects and their yarns

THE SHOES

Ballet Flats
Sirdar Snuggly Baby Bamboo DK (80% bamboo, 20% wool): Jolly Spicy Red (173)

Daisy Chain Mary Janes
MC Patons DK (100% cotton): Apple (2205)
CC Sirdar Snuggly Baby Bamboo DK (80% bamboo, 20% wool): Cream (131); Rowan Baby Merino Silk DK (66% merino wool, 34% silk): Limone (675)

Classic Slip-ons
MC Sirdar Simply Recycled DK (51% cotton, 49% acrylic): Denim Wash (016)
CC Sirdar Simply Recycled DK (51% cotton, 49% acrylic): Chalk White (010)

Point Shoes
Patons Smoothie DK (100% acrylic): Apricot (2004)

Brogues
MC Sirdar Snuggly Baby Bamboo DK(80% bamboo, 20% wool): Cream (131)
CC Patons 4-ply (100% cotton): Chocolate (1162)

Cutwork Shoes
Rowan Kid Classic Aran (70% wool, 26% mohair, 4% nylon): Feather (828)

Cherry Slippers
MC Sirdar Snuggly Baby Bamboo DK (80% bamboo, 20% wool): Cream (131)
CC Patons DK (100% cotton): Apple (2205); Sirdar Snuggly Baby Bamboo DK (80% bamboo, 20% wool): Jolly Spicy Red (173)

Rosebud Party Pumps
MC Sirdar Simply Recycled DK (51% cotton, 49% acrylic): Pumice (021)
CC Sirdar Simply Recycled DK (51% cotton, 49% acrylic): Seashells (017)

Molded Clogs
King Cole Cottonsoft DK (100% cotton): Mint (715)

Moccasins
MC Rowan Pure Wool DK (100% wool): Tan (054)
CC Rowan 4-ply (50% merino wool, 50% cotton): String (481)

THE BOOTS

Vintage Bow Boots
MC Sirdar Simply Recycled DK (51% cotton, 49% acrylic): Seashells (017)
CC Sirdar Simply Recycled DK (51% cotton, 49% acrylic): Canvas (011)

Button Boots
Sirdar Simply Recycled DK (51% recycled cotton, 49% acrylic): Pumice (021)

Cowboy Boots
MC Rowan DK (50% merino wool, 50% cotton): Cafe (985)
CC Patons DK (100% cotton): Chocolate (2162); Patons DK (100% cotton): Silver (2172)

Furry Boots
MC Rowan Cotton Glace DK (100% cotton): Toffee (843)
CC Rowan Cotton Glace DK (100% cotton): Oyster (730)

Desert Boots
MC Sirdar Simply Recycled Aran: Raffia (0034)
CC Rowan Pure Wool DK (100% wool): Anthracite (003)

Fringed Boots
MC Sirdar Simply Recycled DK (51% cotton, 49% acrylic): Clay (0011)
CC Rowan Cotton Glace DK (100% cotton): Oyster (730)

Baseball Boots
MC Sirdar Snuggly Baby Bamboo DK (80% bamboo, 20% wool): Jolly Spicy Red (173)
CC Sirdar Snuggly Baby Bamboo DK (80% bamboo, 20% wool): Cream (131)

Biker Boots
MC Patons DK (100% cotton): Chocolate (2162)

Snow Boots
MC Patons Diploma Gold DK (55% wool, 25% acrylic, 20% nylon): Bright Aqua (06243)
CC Rowan Pure Wool DK (100% wool): Anthracite (003)

Work Boots
MC Rowan DK (50% merino wool, 50% cotton): Brolly (980)
CC Patons DK (100% cotton): Chocolate (2162)

THE SANDALS
Jelly Sandals
Rowan Baby Merino Silk DK (66% merino wool, 34% silk): Limone (675)

Grecian Sandals
MC Patons DK (100% cotton): Silver (2172)
CC Sirdar Simply Recycled DK (51% recycled cotton, 49% acrylic): Canvas (011)

Bow Front Sandals
DMC Natura Just Cotton 4-ply (100% cotton): Amaranto (N33)

Woven Leather Sandals
Sirdar Simply Recycled Aran: Raffia (0034)

Ruffle Front Sandals
MC Patons Smoothie DK (100% acrylic): Apricot (2004)
CC Rowan Pure Wool DK (100% wool): Anthracite (003)

Comfort Sandals
MC Sirdar Simply Recycled DK (51% recycled cotton, 49% acrylic): Greenhouse (014)
CC Sirdar Simply Recycled DK (51% recycled cotton, 49% acrylic): Cork (012)

Espadrilles
MC Rowan Cotton Glace DK (100% cotton): Oyster (730)
CC Sirdar Snuggly Baby Bamboo DK (80% bamboo, 20% wool): Jolly Spicy Red (173)

Flowery Sandals
MC Sirdar Simply Recycled DK (51% cotton, 49% acrylic): cork (012)
CC Patons DK (100% cotton): Apple (2205); Sirdar Simply Recycled DK (51% cotton, 49% acrylic): Seashells (017)

Pom-Pom Slippers
Sirdar Snuggly Baby Cotton DK (100% cotton): Bo Peep Pink (156)

Gladiator Sandals
MC Sirdar Simply Recycled DK (51% cotton, 49% acrylic): Cork (012)
CC Sirdar Simply Recycled Aran: Raffia (0034)

Author acknowledgments
I would like to thank Caroline Smith who offered me this opportunity after reading my interview in **Inside Crochet** magazine. I would also like to thank Claire Montgomerie (the editor of **Inside Crochet** magazine) for that interview. I would like to thank the Quantum team—Samantha Warrington, Hazel Eriksson, and Luise Roberts who worked on this book with me; Anna Southgate for her editorial support; and Blanche Williams for designing the book. I would like to thank my family for their help and encouragement during this work— my mom, my brother, my husband. I would like to thank my grandmother who taught me to crochet. And I would like to thank my children, Sophie and Alexandre, for being my greatest inspiration.

To see more of Vita's designs, visit her website at http://monpetitviolon.com

index